30 DAYS TO MAKING MONEY ONLINE

SIMPLE STEPS TO SOLVING THE ONLINE SALES PUZZLE

Internet Sales Mastery Academy ™

CHAPTER 1: THE SUCCESS MIND-SET 9
- THE MIND-SET RESET 9
- WHAT DEFINES SUCCESS? 10
- WHAT IS SUCCESS FOR YOU? WHAT WOULD A SUCCESSFUL LIFESTYLE LOOK LIKE TO YOU? 13
- WHAT DEFINES FAILURE? 13
- ELIMINATING NEGATIVE QUESTIONS 14
- WHAT ARE THE QUESTIONS YOU HAVE BEEN ASKING YOURSELF? 16
- WHAT'S YOUR "WHY"? 19
- DEFINE YOUR VALUES! 21
- SETTING YOUR GOALS 24
- YOUR GOAL SETTING MAP 25
- WHAT ARE YOUR TOP 100 GOALS? 25
- HOW WOULD YOU FEEL IF YOU ACHIEVED ALL OF YOUR GOALS? 26
- TAKING ACTION 27
- WHAT DO YOU NEED TO DO? 27
- WHAT THINGS NEED TO BE CHANGED? 28
- THE PATH TO CHANGE 29
- GETTING OUT OF YOUR COMFORT ZONE BY MOVING INTO THE ZONE 29
- WHAT DO YOU NEED TO STOP OR START DOING? 31
- WHO DO YOU NEED ON YOUR TEAM? 31
- WHAT SYSTEMS WILL YOU NEED TO HAVE IN PLACE? 32
- FIND A MENTOR OR A PERSONAL COACH 33
- RITUALS 34

CHAPTER 2: WHAT SELLS? 39
- INTRODUCTION 39
- KEY AREAS OF RESEARCH 40
- THE NICHE MARKET 41
- FINDING TOP SELLERS 41
- RESEARCHING TRENDS 44
- IDENTIFY THE PROBLEM, SOLVE THE PROBLEM, SELL THE SOLUTION 46
- SURVEY YOUR CUSTOMERS 49

CHAPTER 3: KNOW THY CUSTOMER 53
- IDENTIFYING YOUR CUSTOMER: THE RESEARCH PHASE 54
- GOOGLE 54
- FACEBOOK 55

 Alexa.com 58
 Comparative Analysis 59
 Your Customer Avatar 60
 Creating Your Dream Customer Avatar 60
 The Trader Joe's Customer Avatar 62
 Why Have an Avatar? 63

CHAPTER 4: TESTING THE WATERS 67
 Will It Sell? 67
 Amazon 68
 eBay 69
 Etsy and Quirky 69
 ClickBank, WarriorForum, and Udemy 69
 Indiegogo and Kickstarter Crowdfunding 70
 TeeSpring, CustomInk, Skreened, Gearbubble 70
 Clarity, Craigslist, Angieslist, oDesk, and Elance 71
 The Sales Process 72
 Writing Item Descriptions 73
 Post-Sales and Customer Service 74
 Don't Fall in Love! 76

CHAPTER 5: SETTING UP YOUR ONLINE PRESENCE 81
 The Pre-Build 82
 Points of Analysis 89
 Testing Your Competitors 90
 Domain Name Selection 91
 Web Hosting 92
 Design and Build 93
 Design 95
 Colors 95
 Web Design Resources 97
 Logo Design 97
 Custom Site Design Templates 97
 Images 97
 eCommerce Store Setup 98
 Email Automation 98
 Testing 99

CHAPTER 6: MARKETING 103

CREATING THE SALES MESSAGE 104
HONING YOUR MESSAGE 109
   THE HEADLINE 109
   THE IRRESISTIBLE OFFER 110
   BULLET POINTS 112
   GUARANTEE AND TRIAL PERIOD 113
   REVIEWS AND TESTIMONIALS 113
   ALWAYS USE A CALL TO ACTION 114
   VIDEO 115
   SPLIT-TEST EVERYTHING 116
GO TO WHERE YOUR CUSTOMER IS 117
   FACEBOOK 118
   LINKEDIN 119
   GOOGLE+ 120
   TWITTER 120
   YOUTUBE 121
   PINTEREST 123
   INSTAGRAM 124
   YELP 124
   PODCASTING 124
SOCIAL MEDIA BEST PRACTICES 125
   DESIGN AND MESSAGE CONGRUENCY 127
   ADVERTISING 128
   FACEBOOK ADVERTISING 128
   GOOGLE PAID SEARCH 131
   SETTING UP YOUR GOOGLE AD 132
   NEGATIVE KEYWORDS 135
   RETARGETING 136
   EMAIL MARKETING 137
   THE SUBJECT LINE 138
   THE MESSAGE 139
   REENGAGING OLD PROSPECTS OR CUSTOMERS 140
   EMAIL LIST BUILDING 141
   LANDING AND SQUEEZE PAGES 142
   PERFORMANCE TRACKING 143
   CAMPAIGNS VS. ONE-OFF ADS AND EMAILS 143
OFFLINE MARKETING 144

CHAPTER 7: CREATING SALES SUCCESS 149
PRESENTING YOUR OFFER 150
UNCOVER YOUR UNIQUE SELLING PROPOSITION (USP) 151
SELLING 152
REMARKETING 152
KEEP SELLING TO EXISTING CUSTOMERS 153
SHOPPING CART ABANDONMENT REMARKETING 154
BUYING TRIGGERS, WHAT REALLY MAKES PEOPLE BUY 155
ANTICIPATION 155
SOCIAL PROOF 156
MEDIA 156
SCARCITY 157
EXPAND YOUR OFFER OPTIONS 159
ENTRY-LEVEL PRODUCTS 159
PRODUCT BUNDLING 159
OVERCOMING OBJECTIONS 160
FAQ 161
REMOVING RISK 161
GUARANTEE AND TRIAL PERIODS 162
SECURITY BADGES 163

CHAPTER 8: THE RAVING FAN CUSTOMER 167
CREATING RAVING FAN CUSTOMERS 167
DESIGNING YOUR CUSTOMER EXPERIENCE TOUCH POINTS 169
PRE-SALES TOUCH POINTS 170
DURING-SALES TOUCH POINTS 171
DELIVERY TOUCH POINTS 171
TESTIMONIALS AND REFERRALS 175
SETTING UP YOUR TOUCH POINTS 175

Copyright © 2017 Internet Sales Mastery. Internet Sales Mastery Academy. All rights reserved. No part of this document may be reproduced in any form, including photocopying or transmission electronically to any computer, without the prior written consent of ISM. The information contained in this document is proprietary to ISM, and may not be used or disclosed except as expressly authorized in writing by ISM.

Introduction

Are you thinking of selling online but have no clue where to start? Or are you already selling online, and you want to take your business to the next level? In this book, I'll teach you everything it takes to succeed with an online business . . . and more . . .

Back in 1994, I got my first computer, and shortly after that, I started designing web pages for myself. At the time I was a successful photographer in NYC, making a living shooting for clients like Revlon and Nicole Miller, shooting all the "super models" of the day. I realized the potential that the Internet was opening up, and soon after buying my first Mac, I lost my passion for photography and started my love affair with the Internet and computers.

After getting out of the photography business, I moved to New Mexico and opened up a small web design firm. I was lucky enough to have a thriving little business serving fashion and photography clients in NYC. I was living a dream life. I was being paid NYC rates, while living in NM, one cheapest states in the entire USA. I had to work only a few days a month, and I was set, with a lifestyle I could only have dreamed of when living in NYC.

I was always exploring ways to make money online. I had been dabbling with eBay, selling the cameras I no longer needed, and I started test-selling items I bought at Walmart. To my amazement, people bought those Walmart items, and I made a nice profit!

Then 9/11 happened, and in a span of three months I lost all of my clients … one by one. I looked at my bank account and discovered that I had only a hundred dollars left!!! I had no idea what to do. There were no jobs in New Mexico to speak of that I would qualify for, so I

Introduction

had to get creative and come up with a quick solution in order to pay my bills. I needed to make some money. I needed to turn my life around.

I thought the easiest way to make some fast money would probably be to list some stuff I didn't need on eBay. I had recently bought a shiny new white iPod, and I knew that if I sold my beloved new toy on eBay, I would have the money I needed to pay off my car insurance before they reported me to the DMV. So I listed the iPod, and I was surprised that it sold in less than a day. The person who bought it paid me immediately. I was saved! The problem was, I had listed it "As Good As New," because it was less than eight weeks old, but I had failed to check it before I listed it. When I finally located my iPod in the bottom of a backpack, I saw that it had taken a total beating and was far from new looking. I was screwed! Or so I thought.

What happened next changed my life. I had two choices: I could cancel the sale and send the money back, or I could find a solution to the problem. Sending the money back was not an option, so I jumped onto Google and started searching.

I was shocked that there was no product on the market to fix this simple problem. Yet some people had posted a few random solutions on user forums about how to get rid of the scratches. The solutions ranged from toothpaste to car polishes.

Eventually, I found a solution that looked promising. Immediately, a light bulb went off in my head. But first I had to test it to see whether it worked, so I ran down to the local auto parts store and bought a few polishes and mixed them up. It worked like a dream! Within a few minutes, my iPod looked like new. I was saved, I did not have to send the money back, and I could pay off some of my bills!

Introduction

As I had enough polishing liquid left to fix another 999 iPods, I decided to test the silly idea I'd had earlier. I came up with a catchy name, "iCleaner," and designed a quick logo, printed it onto an address sticker, and stuck it on a bottle. I then took a photo of it and listed it on eBay, explaining what this miracle liquid would do to your scratched iPod. I put a "Buy it now" price of $9 (the cost of all the products I had bought) + $2.50 for shipping and hit the "submit" button.

Initially, I thought it would just be a good joke to laugh about someday, but when I went back to my computer an hour later, it had sold! So I relisted it, and once again I sold another one in less than an hour! I kept relisting it, and by 9 p.m., I had sold five more. People started to ask all kinds of questions, so, to answer them all at once, I decided to put up a quick one-page website with my new "product," a brief description of what the product did, with before and after photos, and a "Buy it now" button.

When I woke up the next morning, I ran down to my computer to see whether I had sold anything on eBay. Once again, I was amazed that I had sold another bottle of iCleaner! But now I felt stupid for having put up only a single item. I should have listed ten or more. When I looked at my email, though, I had ten sales from my single-page website, because people who could not buy it on eBay went to my website and bought there.

I was officially in business!

Long story cut short ... within a few days, I had distributors from Australia contacting me, in three months I was selling all over the world, and in less than four years I retired.

I had started my business with only $9!

I have since sold everything from houses to books and motorcyles, all

Introduction

the way to part of my 320 acre ranch, online.

Along the way, I made many mistakes, but thankfully I learned from each and every one. I was able to turn each mistake around and reap huge benefits. When I first started my online business, I worked eighteen-hour days . . . but it never felt like work because it truly was some of the most fun I have ever had.

I have had the freedom to travel the world, have been to all seven continents twice, and have visited more than 118 countries. I meet some of the most amazing people on this planet, from beggars and monks to millionaires and billionaires. I have learned lessons from all of them.

I have also had the pleasure to meet and work with some of the best marketers in the world, people who have made tens of millions in a single day with their online businesses. I took notes from all of these marketers, and in this book I have combined the best strategies that they and I use.

Through my online business, I was able to change my life, and now it is my mission to help others do the same.

I hope this book will encourage you to take that first step toward making your life as great as it can be.

Remember, as long as you still have a few dollars in your pocket and the will to work hard, you can start a successful online business and change your life forever.

Preface

When it comes to starting up new businesses anywhere, online or offline, the statistics are rather grim. About 50 percent of all new businesses fail by the fourth year after their inception, and by their tenth year, only 29 percent will still be around! That means 71 percent will have failed!

More often than not, new businesses fail!

You basically have a much better chance at making money by gambling in a Las Vegas casino than you have by starting up your own business!

Your motivation for starting an online business can vary. Some people start up a business after they get laid off; others are sick and tired of working for someone else nine to five and want more independence. Some individuals want more free time, or they may want to work from home to spend more time with their families. For some of you, it may be a lifelong dream that you just haven't gotten around to pursuing yet.

If you are looking for more free time, all I can say right now is that you won't be getting it anytime soon. Starting up a new business will take a lot of hard work and long hours. You'll probably have to work harder than you ever have and spend more time doing so.

Until you get the systems down and start to make money and can outsource what you aren't willing to do yourself, it's going to take everything you have. Your patience, creativity, and endurance will all be taken to their limit, so be ready!

Lots of budding entrepreneurs believe that working in a certain field for a few years gives them sufficient expertise and experience to run their own business. Yet the truth is, most people starting a new business venture have no idea what it really takes to succeed. Creating a successful online business requires much more than just dreaming up a business plan, buying some inventory, and setting up a fancy website, then hoping that people will show up and buy.

Sooner or later, most newbie online entrepreneurs wake up to the reality that they are working harder and more hours than they ever have before, for less than the minimum wage. They realize that the sales on their website are not covering their costs. Then they go into panic mode and spend their last cash reserves on random advertising attempts or buy into some online guru's latest traffic-generation system. They eventually fail, end up shutting down their website, go out of business, and go back to their 9 to 5 jobs.

That starts the blame game. They may blame their business's failure on difficult economic times, on not having a large-enough marketing budget, or on some other external factor. While some of these factors may have had an influence on the demise of a business, the real truth is that no matter how bad the economy is or how small your startup budget is, you can succeed online as long as you have the right mind-set and the correct knowledge.

Some of the biggest and most successful companies in the world were started during a recession. Apple, Microsoft, General Electric, Fed Ex, and Disney are all giants in their industries now, but they defied the odds, were established during a recession, and succeeded.

In this book, I will walk you through proven steps that you need to take in order to avoid the pitfalls of failure, and I will guide you on a clear path toward success.

Your decisions control the destiny of your life. Becoming successful is a matter of strategy and correct knowledge, but, above all, it is your mind-set. Your mind-set will control the decisions that you make to create your success. It's our decisions, not our conditions, that control our destiny.

The path to success is to take bold, determined action with the right mind-set. For this reason, in the first chapter of this book, we will concentrate on developing your success mind-set.

Chapter 1: The Success Mind-Set

The Mind-Set Reset

With the right mind-set, you can overcome almost any obstacle or problem. Skills and experience are crucial elements, but your mind-set will contribute the most toward your long-term success.

One reason so few of us achieve what we truly want in our lives is that we never direct our focus. We never concentrate our power on what matters to us. Many of us don't even know what we really want. Most people dabble their way through life, never deciding to master anything in particular, and they never even ask themselves life's basic questions.

Most people never think about what they want out of life, nor have they clarified what a perfect life looks like to them. Many times, I have posed a simple question to people who are looking for a better life: What would a perfect life look like to you? And they can't answer it. So then I ask them: What would a perfect day look like to you? They gradually come up with some answers.

You see, most of the time we get caught up in grand visions of something better, but we really do not know what we want. We focus on our current situation and on what is not working, and we get stuck there. The reason this happens is because whatever we focus our energy on, we get more of.

So if you are focusing on problems in life or in your business or are dwelling on what you don't want, sadly that is what you will get more of. The trick is to focus on what you want more of and on finding a solution for how to get there.
In this chapter, you will learn how to change your thinking and how to be aware of what you are thinking. You will also learn a system for how to set goals to attain anything in life, so that you can achieve success and change your life forever.

What Defines Success?

Before you can embark on a journey toward success, you must know what it really means to you. For some people, success may be accumulating wealth and expensive cars and living a "celebrity lifestyle," while to others, it may be having the freedom to do whatever they want, when they want to. Or maybe all you want is simply to spend time with loved ones and live a lifestyle you can afford and enjoy without worries.

To create lasting success, you must connect to your OWN ambition.

Many people are not living by their own standards, but by standards and ideas that others have set for them. Maybe their family or friends told them what they should be focusing their efforts on.

Chapter 1

Maybe they just took a job because it was the only one available at the time, and it seemed like a good, easy way to pay the bills. Are you one of these people? Most of the time, we are in denial about the possibility that we are not living our own version of life but are living a version that others have imposed on us or a life that is simply the easy way out.

Are you really living your dream life, or is it a dream life by someone else's standards? Are you really working in a dream job, or is it a dream job by someone else's standards? Are you following your own vision in life, or are you walking in someone else's footsteps? Is this really the life you were destined for?

Remember the simple questions I asked before: What does a perfect day look like to you? What would your perfect life look like? Take a break from reading and spend some time thinking about this.

I ask you this because many of us are attempting to live according to everyone's critiques of us and plans for us, which is like chasing a pot of gold at the end of the rainbow. It's just not a realistic possibility. We may think it would be a great treasure to have everyone's approval, but it's an ever-elusive journey to insanity. You can drive yourself insane trying to meet everyone's expectations.

The best expectations to meet are your own, regarding what you want to do most with your life. Follow your feelings, not others' ideas, to help you decide what you should do. THAT'S where you'll find your success.

What are your personal definitions of success? What makes someone successful in your mind? Is it having a lot of money? Does it mean having a big house? An expensive car? Or is it simply being out of debt? Or being your own boss? Where do you see yourself a year from now? Where do you see yourself ten years from now? What do you want to become? Who do you want to become? What do you want in your life?

To gain total clarity, pull out a piece of paper or a notebook and take a few minutes to write down your answers. The reason I want you to write the answers, instead of simply thinking of them, is that when you write, you gain more clarity, and it helps expand your awareness and boosts your cognition.

Start with something easy. What would a perfect day look like to you?

As simple as this sounds, it's a great way to gain clarity about what has meaning for you, what lifestyle you really want to have. Once you have visualized this day, write down every little detail. What do you want to create? What do you want to do? Who do you want to be?

The reason I like to start with such a simple vision is because the simpler you make your beginning with anything in life, the quicker you build momentum in creating whatever you like.

Design your days, design your weeks, design your years…design your life.

Once you have gotten clear about what an ideal day looks like to you, I would like you to take some further steps by deciding what a great week would look like . . . and so forth, until you can envision what an amazing life looks like. The better you can envision your future, the more likely that it will become reality. See who you are going to be . . . see what is going to be in your life.

Chapter 1

What Is Success for You? What Would a Successful Lifestyle Look Like to You?

The more detailed you are in answering these questions, the better you will know where to focus your energy, and the sooner you will actually embark on the road to success.

Is your vision of a successful life having luxurious possessions, along with fame and power? Is it having freedom and autonomy in all of your choices in life? Or maybe you want to spend more time with your family? What do you really want in your life?

Success is a moving target, so it's important to know when you are succeeding, in order to feel a sense of accomplishment and fulfillment. Without having a clear marker for knowing when you are successful or succeeding, you can end up feeling empty and unfulfilled. Then you might sabotage your path to success and may even give up entirely. Think about the answer to this question: When will you know that you are successful?

What Defines Failure?

Once you have identified your vision of success, you should establish a dichotomous balance. What is failure to you? Is it lack of money? Being in debt? Not achieving your goals? Not having free time to spend with your loved ones? Being unhealthy? Being overweight?

When you determine your definition of failure, you will know what to steer clear of, by being aware when you are heading in the wrong direction.

The clearer you can answer these questions, the higher your chance of success will be. Knowing what you want to avoid and steer clear of is key to gaining control of your success. Once you know what *not* to focus on, you will discover what *you must* focus on.

Whatever you set your focus on in life is what you get more of in life. So you need to stop focusing on what you *don't* want in your life, and start focusing on what you *do* want.

What obstacles do you need to overcome in your life in order to succeed?

Many times, knowing what NOT to focus on is just as important or even more important than knowing what *to* focus on, so take some time right now to think about what you should NOT be focusing on!

Eliminating Negative Questions

Everything you do is based on choices you make. Your choices are based on questions you ask yourself. Most of us don't even realize that we are subconsciously asking ourselves questions on a continuous basis. Most of our actions or inactions in life occur in reaction to our internal dialogue: the questions we ask ourselves and the way we answer them. Our lives are filled with questions.

Successful people ask better questions, and, as a result, they get better answers.

Consider whether you have asked yourself one of the following questions in the last few months:

Why does this always happen to me? What is wrong with me? Why do others have all the luck?
Why does nothing good ever happen to me? When will I be out of this mess?

Chapter 1

We, as humans, are prone to fall into repetitive habits, which ultimately gain control over our lives. This happens with questions as well. There is a series of questions that we tend to ask ourselves over and again.

Questions can be the most powerful motivators in our lives, but if you ask the wrong question, you will end up being unmotivated and will focus on things that won't help you get ahead in life. All of the above questions are disempowering. All of them will give you a justification for a problem; none of them will give you a positive answer that points toward a solution.

When you ask yourself questions, make sure these are questions with answers you can take action on. The above questions do not empower the thinker to take further action in an effective direction.

When you have tuned in to a negative mind-set, your mind will not only create negative answers to these questions but will also condition you to accept the answers without reproach or argument. The answers that your mind delivers to you are an attempt to convince you that you lack the skills, the drive, the finances, or the experience to succeed. Each statement your mind comes up with will create barriers to stop you from taking positive action toward your success. It is your job to ignore any questions that disempower you and to create and replace them with questions that empower you.

Take a few moments to think about questions you ask yourself on a regular basis. Are there any you have asked yourself over and over again? Which ones? Remember, you may be aware that you ask yourself these questions, but more likely you have been totally unaware . . . that is, until now.

What Are the Questions You Have Been Asking Yourself?

Do the questions you ask seem to give you a solution? Or do they disempower you and the answers give you a bunch of excuses and justifications? If you are asking yourself this kind of question, you need to STOP immediately!! These questions are probably the biggest factor that is holding you back on your path to success and wealth.

You need to begin reprogramming your standard response when something does not go the way you think it should. You need to replace those disempowering questions with better-quality questions that serve you, by finding empowering answers and solutions.

But how do you do stop asking yourself disempowering questions?

First, you need to identify the key questions you keep asking yourself, over and over again. To do this, go back and think about a situation where you were challenged and you failed. What was the situation like when you asked yourself these questions? Write it down. Next, see if you can find other situations where you failed, and think about the questions you asked yourself. Do you see a pattern? Are the questions the same or similar? Is there one question you keep on asking yourself that stands out, apart from the rest?

It is this one question that I call the "Key Question." We want to change it and switch it around, so that it becomes a question whose answer empowers you to take action and find solutions and a positive outcome. So, think about that situation. Think of a question you could ask yourself that could empower you to find a solution.

The key to transforming your question is to change your questions so that the answers to them become empowering and lead to positive solutions. Through this change, you will place yourself in an active position, rather than a passive one. Notice that the following sentences have positioned you as the recipient of events or conditions that were beyond your control, whereas the new questions put control of the outcome into your hands.

Bad Question:
"Why does this always happen to me?"
Better Question:
"How can I take full advantage of this situation and make the best of it?"

Bad Question:
"Why am I not good enough?"
Better Question:
"How can I get even better so that more great things happen to me?"
Bad Question:
"What's wrong with me?"
Better Question:
"How can I appreciate even more everything that's right with me?"

Bad Question:
"When will things go right for me?"
Better Question:
"What can I do today to achieve my goals to gain even greater success?"

By asking yourself questions that give you an empowered point of view, you will develop the innate ability to look for solutions and not problems. Remember, nature has its job to do, too. In fact, being empowered will help with your reactions to what happens to you. The decision to be empowered is on you. You have to think consciously, choose, and decide how you want to feel about anything happening in your life.

What can I learn from this situation? What do I want to accomplish? What is the most effective thing I can focus on? How can I improve on my skills? What would a better solution be? What are my options, really?

What was the old "Key Question" you had been asking yourself? What would a better new "Key Question" be for you?

Sit down and write your answers to the following: Think about how you can use your old Key Question as the basis to make the switch. What actions, feelings, or emotions were you trying to fulfill with the old question? How can you switch it to a more positive question? What were you able to avoid with your old question? What would the opposite of that be?

You want your new question to have precisely the opposite effect of its old negative counterpart. While disempowering questions focus your mind on what you don't have, can't do, and are not—and therefore take away your power to act—empowering questions focus your mind what you have, what you can do, and who you really are.

Take some time to really analyze your answers. When you brainstorm on paper, you get better insight into what your real thoughts are. Take time to figure out all of the meanings behind your old question, and write your new question so that it creates positive solutions and gets you to take positive actions that will help you on your path to success.

After you have your new Key Question, you must turn it into a mantra.

Once you have selected and written down your new "Key Question," you should repeat it about fifty times in a row to make sure that it really is empowering and feels right to you. Tweak it, if necessary, so that it starts to become second nature to you, so that it flows from you without resistance. Then print it out as a poster, and hang it in your office, kitchen, or car, someplace where you will constantly be reminded of it. Keep a small copy of it as a card in your wallet or as your desktop wallpaper on your computer.

Repeat it a few times before you go to sleep every night and also a few times when you wake up in the morning for a week or so. The main idea is to keep it in mind and in a visible location where you will come across it on a daily basis.

Soon you will find that the old negative question you had been asking yourself over and over again will be replaced by the new positive Key Question. You will start to notice that you are reacting in different ways and taking different actions than you did before.

In theory, it's easy to undermine this strategy by calling it simplistic and idealistic. Yet on the contrary, making small changes in your subconscious behavior will open the doors to your ultimate success.

Once your subconscious mind starts asking you your new Key Question, you will deliver actions in the form of answers. This strategy of tackling problems will then trickle down through your life, resulting in long-term success.

What's Your "Why"?

Most people do not follow through on taking action or on pursuing their dreams for one main reason: they do not have a strong enough WHY! Our "why" is our strongest motivator for change. It is the reason behind all of our actions and thoughts. In order to succeed, we need to make sure that our "why" is as strong as possible.

By now, you will have identified your definitions of success and failure on a personal and professional level. You now need to delve deeper into your heart to understand why you want to achieve your own brand of success. Don't settle for an answer on the surface, but, rather, allow it to lead you toward a deeper meaning until you understand why success matters to you.

The motivating factor that you identify at this point should be strong enough to help you move forward and take action when it is needed.

Many times, we are "confused" about the reason we actually are or are not motivated to take a certain action. This is because we have not really looked into the true reason behind why we want certain things. Most people think they want to start a business because they want to have more money or free time, and the reason they don't succeed is that this is the superficial "why" of their motivation. We are all guided by our value systems in our lives. Values are the force that drives and shapes all of our emotions, our actions, our quality of life, and, ultimately, our destiny.

Your values are the things you believe are important in the way you live and work.

They should determine your priorities, and, deep down, they're probably the yardstick you use to measure whether your life is turning out the way you want it to.

When your actions and the way you behave match your values, life is usually good—you're satisfied and content. But when these don't align with your values, that's when things feel . . . wrong. This can be a real source of unhappiness and lack of motivation to take action.

This is why making a conscious effort to identify and define your values is so important.

Define Your Values!

When you define your values, you discover what's truly important to you. A good way to start doing this is by looking back on your life: identifying when you felt good and were confident that you were making good choices.

First, identify the times when you were happiest. Find examples from both your career and your personal life. This will ensure some balance in your answers.

What were you doing? Were you with other people? Who? What other factors contributed to your happiness?

After you have done that, identify the times when you were proudest. And once again, use examples from your career and personal life to pinpoint these.

Why were you proud? Did other people share your pride? Who? What other factors contributed to your feelings of pride?

Next, identify the times when you were most fulfilled and satisfied. Again, use both personal and work examples.

What need or desire was fulfilled? How and why did the experience give your life meaning? What other factors contributed to your feelings of fulfillment?

Now, determine your top values, based on your experiences of happiness, pride, and fulfillment.

Why is each experience truly important and memorable? Use the list of common personal values in Fig. 1.1 to help you get started—and aim for about ten top values. (As you work through the list, you may find that some of these values naturally combine. For instance, if you value philanthropy, community, and generosity, you might say that service to others is one of your top values.)

And finally, prioritize your top values.

This step is probably the most difficult, because you'll have to look deep inside yourself. It's also the most important step, because, when making a decision, you'll have to choose between solutions that may satisfy different values. This is when you must know which value is more important to you.

Write down your top ten values, not in any particular order.

Look at the first two values and ask yourself, "If I could satisfy only one of these, which would I choose?" It might help to visualize a situation in which you would have to make that choice. For example, if you compare the values of service and stability, imagine that you must decide whether to start a new business or keep your current job at a hospital. Keep working through the list, by comparing each value with every other value, until your list is in the correct order.

Knowing your values and having them in order will give you a system to ensure that what you are doing will be in line with your actual "why." Being aware of your correct values gives you a strong WHY, which will motivate you to follow through on your vision, even in the toughest situations!

Chapter 1

Accountability	Excellence	Order
Accuracy	Expertise	Originality
Achievement	Exploration	Patriotism
Adventurousness	Expressiveness	Perfection
Altruism	Fairness	Piety
Ambition	Faith	Positivity
Assertiveness	Fidelity	Practicality
Authenticity	Fitness	Preparedness
Balance	Focus	Professionalism
Belonging	Free	Prudence
Boldness	Fun	Resourcefulness
Calmness	Generosity	Restraint
Carefulness	Goodness	Results-oriented
Challenge	Grace	Rigor
Commitment	Growth	Security
Community	Happiness	Self-actualization
Compassion	Hard work	Self-control
Consistency	Health	Sensitivity
Contentment	Helping	Serenity
Contribution	Holiness	Service
Control	Honesty	Stability
Cooperation	Honor	Strategy
Correctness	Humility	Strength
Creativity	Independence	Structure
Decisiveness	Ingenuity	Success
Dependability	Inquisitiveness	Support
Determination	Insightfulness	Teamwork
Devoutness	Intelligence	Thankful
Diligence	Joy	Thorough
Effectiveness	Justice	Timeliness
Efficiency	Leadership	Traditionalism
Elegance	Legacy	Unique
Empathy	Love	Usefulness
Enjoyment	Loyalty	Value
Enthusiasm	Mastery	Youth
Equality	Obedience	Young
	Openness	Zest

FIG. 1.1

Setting Your Goals

Setting goals is the first step in turning the invisible into the visible.

Goals are a key factor in success, not only in your personal life but also in your business.

Many studies have been conducted on goal setting. One of my favorites was done with Harvard graduates a few years ago, in which they asked the students what their goals were after graduating. Amazingly enough, 84 percent of the Harvard graduates had never even thought about their goals. They had no clear idea of what they really wanted in their lives. Only 16 percent of the graduates had taken the time to think about what their goals were, and only 3 percent had actually written down their goals.

What's truly astounding is that when the researchers checked back with the graduates ten years later, they found that those who had goals earned more than double the amount of those who had not. What is even more unbelievable is that graduates who had written down their goals earned ten times as much as those who didn't have any goals!

When did you last set goals? Most people think about goals or make New Year's resolutions on December 31 and then forget about them. Did you make New Year's resolutions? Did you want to lose weight . . . stop smoking? Get out of debt? Make more money? Get a new job?

How did you do? Did you stick with it? Do you even remember what your New Year's resolutions were? Is it because your resolutions were not important enough to you? Is it because you lack will power? Was the goal too ambitious or unattainable? Or was it simply that you had a few too many glasses of champagne and forgot about them by the next morning?

The truth is, setting resolutions or goals on New Year's Eve simply doesn't work!! Studies show that 50 percent of people fall back to their old habits before the end of the January, and by the end of the year, only 8 percent have succeeded in attaining their goals!

Very few people take time during the year to set out to achieve the goals they have defined. If you don't think about the goals, you will not take the necessary actions that would lead to toward their completion.

Your Goal Setting MAP

A goal without a plan is only a dream! A Goal Setting MAP (Massive Action Plan) allows you to take control of your life and your goals. In simple terms, you need to get from Point A to Point B, but you also need to have a clear idea of what it will entail.

What Are Your Top 100 Goals?

The first step in this process is to write down what you really want in your life. Go wild, think BIG . . . remember when you were a kid at Christmas time, making a list of things you wanted from Santa? Think of anything you've ever wanted, personally or professionally. For fifteen minutes, I want you to write like crazy, until you have written down at least a hundred goals or wishes. They can be anything: a yacht, a bigger house, being out of debt, a million dollars in the bank, a salary of $10,000 a month, a new job, or losing fifty pounds.

Just write down, as fast as possible, everything you think might be fun to have or what you really want or need in your life right now or in the near and distant future

Once you have a hundred goals written down, you must determine a time frame in which you would like to achieve each goal, so write down the time frame next to each goal—that is, the number of years that you will take to achieve the goal, anywhere from one year to ten years.

Once you have done this, select the top ten one-year goals and write them on a new sheet of paper. Then, next to each one, set a deadline from one to twelve months by which you would like to have achieved each goal.

Next, you are ready to get clear on WHY you really want to achieve each and every goal. Remember what I said before: the main reason people don't follow through on achieving their goals is because they don't have a strong enough WHY. So take your time with this step. Really dig deep into your thoughts, so that you end up with a compelling "why" that will ensure that you follow though and succeed in attaining your goal.

How Would You Feel If You Achieved All of Your Goals?

Visualization is the most important part of this step. Think about how you will feel when you reach the goals you have defined for your life. Don't think only about material things and events that will occur but also consider the emotions you will go through and identify the person you will become.

Now that your goals have started to take shape, ask yourself how you will feel when these goals have been achieved. This will help you map out the internal journey you will need to take and the amount of psychological growth necessary, once you have reached where you want to be.

Now I would like you to visualize a scenario in which you fail and don't achieve your goals, in which you did not take action. Think about the worst that could happen and the way you would feel if you didn't follow through with your plan. Think in terms of the time frame you have set in your head. How important will these goals be to you in the next five years or over the next decade?

How would you feel if you failed to achieve any of your goals?

Once you have visualized yourself failing, think of people around you and determine where they will be in your life should you fail. Think about the worst-case scenario that you can imagine.

Do this in order to raise the stakes. If you have visualized that you stand to lose a lot if you fail to meet your goals, then you will be more likely to achieve them. The more powerful you make your vision of not achieving your goals, the higher the stakes of losing are for you, the more likely it is that you will take action to avoid failing, and the more likely it is you will take steps to actually achieve your goals.

Taking Action

What Do You Need to Do?

First, be very clear about how you will achieve each goal. Take each one-year goal that you have decided on, and break it down into small, single, actionable steps that you will need to take to achieve that goal.

If you want to start an online business, perhaps the small step is registering a domain name, writing up a business plan or a mission statement, or hiring a designer to help you with the design of the website. If you want to lose weight, signing up for a gym, clearing the kitchen of unhealthy foods, or seeing a nutritionist may be one of the first steps you could take.

Move away from extreme all-or-nothing strategies. Too many people think the goal-setting process is over once they declare their goal, and that's when the fun starts. Train your mind to take one small step each day, and you will make amazing progress. It's a process; it's not magic.

Write down each actionable step you need to take for each goal to become reality, and, once again, give it a deadline for when you want to have achieved each step. Then pick the two easiest steps that you can start on right away, put them at the top of your list, and take immediate action on them.

Every great journey starts with one small step, but persistence is what gets you to your final destination!

It may be making a phone call, researching something online, buying a book, or signing up for the gym . . . but it is important that you take a simple action immediately to get the ball rolling! Find that easy step that you can take action on right away and do it. Whatever the step is, make sure you take that first step!! Never set a goal without taking action on it immediately!

What Things Need to Be Changed?

Think about the image of success that you visualized earlier. Is that image drastically different from the way your life is at the moment?

If so, what will you need to do to bring about the change you have visualized, step by step? What are the situations that need to occur? This might also include taking time out to gain clarity of thinking before you choose the next course of action.

NOTE: When you are ready to define the elements that go into creating your MAP, get rid of any distractions you have around you. What you need is a clear-as-crystal vision of what you want, and in that endeavor, distractions will not do. Turn off your cell phone and your computer, and find a quiet place where nobody will interrupt you for about one hour. Pull out a pen and paper so that you can concentrate on creating an amazing future for yourself.

The Path to Change

Achieving your goals isn't just an external process but is also an internal one. Remember, it is all in the mind-set. If your current mind-set isn't getting you where you need to go, what will you need to change?

Do you need to become an action taker? Do you need to change your habits? Do you need to come up with a daily routine or ritual to follow?

Most people do things in their daily lives that they are not even aware of. Most of the time, we do things as if we were set on autopilot. Becoming aware of what you are doing and should not be doing is really the first step toward permanent change.

But how do you actually change a behavior?

Getting Out of Your Comfort Zone by Moving into the Zone

Almost every action we take in life is to either avoid pain or gain pleasure. Most of us live in order to be comfortable and, above all, avoid pain. It's the reason we stay in bad relationships and bad jobs. It's the reason we do not take risks and simply stay in the familiar place that we know best . . . our comfort zone.

There's no room for growth in your comfort zone. In order to grow, you need to truly push your boundaries regarding what is comfortable for you. No one likes to move beyond his or her comfort zone, but that's where the magic happens.

Within your comfort zone, you won't learn new things, experience something exciting, or make the next big step in your career. Only when you get out of your comfort zone will you start to grow.

The problem is that most people let fear get the best of them. They live in a world of fear, worried about failure and loss.

There are a lot of things we would really like to do or that we really should do, but because they are out of our comfort zone, we never get around to doing them. As we start to leave our comfort zone, the feeling of nervousness or anxiety can become so strong that most of us surrender to this feeling and don't talk to the important investor, stop the beautiful girl, or go to the party where we don't know anybody. So if you want to experience crazy shit, feel strong emotions, grow personally, and rev up your career, you'd better start stepping out of your comfort zone.

Become comfortable with taking risks. Your comfort zone is comfortable because it's where you know what to expect. Going out on a limb can be scary because you might fail. You might lose something. But you might also gain something. In order to become comfortable with that uncertainty, you'll need to practice the following.

When is the last time you felt excited about not knowing what was going to happen next? If you're deep in your comfort zone, it's probably been a while. Don't you miss it? Don't you miss the mixture of anticipation and anxiety that makes your heart flutter and stomach turn at the same time? Bring that feeling back into your life.
Do something scary every day! Make a list of things you fear or don't like to do or that scare you. It may be public speaking, heights, or whatever. Start taking action toward eliminating them. You can sign up for toastmasters, go on a tandem skydiving jump . . .

Do whatever it takes to get out of your comfort zone, because life really does begin at the end of your comfort zone, but you will never know unless you step out of it.

Once you start overcoming your fears by stepping out of your comfort zone, you will change your perception of fear, step by step, and instead of **F**inding **E**xcuses **A**nd **R**easons not to step out of your comfort zone, you will **F**eel **E**xcited **A**nd **R**eady to step into the uncomfortable challenge and grow from it!

What Do You Need to Stop or Start Doing?

Many times you can achieve success just by stopping and eliminating bad habits and behaviors. Stop doing things that don't contribute to your overall goals. Negativity, procrastination, overspending, perfectionism, laziness, and overindulging are just some of the most common examples of behavior that could be getting in the way of your success.

What do you need to STOP doing? What do you need to START doing? Make a list of the things you need to start doing. Start doing everything you know you've been neglecting, and stop doing anything that you know will not get you closer to your goals.

Many times, stopping a negative behavior will actually get you further than anything else!

Who Do You Need on Your Team?

If you need to reach someplace, then you have to have a battle plan. In most situations, you will require additional skills to reach where you want to go. You will need a certain type of expertise that you can either learn or hire someone else to do it for you.

If you find yourself procrastinating along the way toward your goal, double-check with yourself to see why you are procrastinating. Ask yourself whether it might be better to outsource that step or process and get someone else to do the job for you more skillfully and faster than you could do it.

Many times, hiring someone else to do tasks you aren't very good at or that you take longer to do will keep the positive momentum flowing until you attain your goal.

What Systems Will You Need to Have in Place?

Consider the tools you will need to help you succeed at attaining your goals.

Many software solutions available on the Internet can help you define your goals in a more streamlined way. Even if you're one of the most dedicated people on earth, it's natural to lose track of your plan, especially in this crazy day and age we live in.
In situations such as these, you will need an external factor to keep you in check. Software solutions such as Wunderlist and OmniFocus or Basecamp, if you are working in a group, will keep tabs on your progress. These software solutions will not only define key dates in your progress but will also contain alarms and deadlines to remind you every step of the way. These tools are great to help you maintain discipline and stay true to your initial goal.

Setting up an accountability system will help you stay on track. Enlist the help of a friend or a family member and initiate the buddy system, where you hold each other accountable and support each other in achieving your goals and deadlines. Designate someone you know and trust to be your referee.

This person will act as an independent third party, monitoring your progress.

If you fail to achieve your goals, set up penalties or punishments so that you have more at stake than simply not achieving the goal itself. Yet also be sure to set up prizes or rewards for achieving your goals, such as a great dinner at your favorite restaurant or gifting yourself a certain item or experience you have wanted for a long time.

You can also use commitment contract websites, such as stickK.com, which offers a contract that binds you into achieving. The contract stipulates that you put money on the line toward donating to an anti-charity or contributing to a political party that you don't support. Having this extra incentive will make achieving your goals even more desirable.

In the end, it all boils down to having a plan and sticking to it. Don't just think about your goal as a vague cloud in the distance. Break it down, think about the semantics, and focus on the details as much as you can. As you watch yourself achieve the smaller goals on your road map, you will see the main goal come closer every day.

Find a Mentor or a Personal Coach

Even with a solid plan and a revitalized sense of purpose, if you have a good source of help, courage, inspiration, and feedback, it can seal the deal.

In the sports world, athletes don't get to the top of their profession without the guidance and support of a coach. Without a coach, they would not be at the peak of their performance and would not achieve success. Coaching can come in many forms—but a coach is someone who will enable you to improve, will motivate you, and will hold you accountable to your goals and enable you to grow. There are many different types of coaches, from personal to business to health coaches.

A good coach can help you identify the gaps between how you'd naturally and comfortably behave and how you need to behave to be effective and speed up your success rate. The coach will give you constructive criticism and advice to improve your weaknesses or to teach you something new and will save you countless hours of frustration, time, and money you would have wasted on doing things by trial and error. A coach will take the guesswork out of what works for your current situation and what does not.

It's not only about how talented you are, but what you can learn from others to help you grow.

Take some time to identify a person in your circle whom you admire—someone who can train you in a new skill or help you grow—or go online and find a coach in the field you need help with. Take a courageous step by reaching out to someone who already embodies the characteristics you would like to emulate. Then witness your weaknesses transform into strengths, simply from asking another person to be your coach.

Rituals

One of the easiest paths to change is to introduce a daily ritual into your life. Successful people have daily rituals that they have thought about and set up in advance and then follow religiously.
When you wake up, normally the stress is already upon you— alarms going off, phones ringing, emails and texts dinging. Before you know it, you are wound up in a situation that you did not want to be in. When you start your day in a reactive mode, you spend the rest of the day reacting, instead of being proactive.

Change your habitual ways. If you start your morning by envisioning what would make the day ahead of you amazing, you can set yourself up for an amazing day. Put yourself in the driver's seat of a perfect day, where you work on your priorities and on whatever will drive your success. This is a better tactic than reacting to what isn't important to you and what won't get you closer to where you want to be.

A trusted morning routine can be extremely effective in helping you be in control and nonreactive. It reduces anxiety and stress and therefore makes you more mindful and competent. Planning out your day in the morning has an enormous effect on your overall efficiency and the rest of your day!

Morning routines are important—but bedtime rituals can have a significant impact on your success.

That's because the very last thing you do before bed affects your mood and energy level the following day, since it often determines how well and how much you sleep.

Gratitude has tremendous power in expanding your happiness. Take some time every night to write down the top three things you are grateful for that happened during the course of the day. This will help you develop a positive mind-set and greater emotional well-being.

Try this: Every night for the next week, set aside a few minutes before you go to sleep. Write down three things that went well that day and why they went well. You may use a journal or your computer to write about the events, but it's important that you have a physical record of what you wrote. The three things need not be earthshaking in significance ("I ran into a long lost friend on the way home from work today"), but they can be important ("I made great progress in learning

French"). Next to each positive event, answer the question "Why did this happen?"

Then, every morning, set aside a few minutes right when you wake up and write down three things that could make that day great. Once again, they can be small things, such as "Add ten minutes to my workout" or "Call Tom, whom I haven't talked to in four months." By doing this, you will start to see incremental changes in the way that you react to situations and will notice that you follow through on your plans, instead of forgetting about them.

If you want to take the whole thing a step further, you can set aside half an hour on Sunday and write down a plan for your coming week. This will strengthen your future vision even more and help you really focus on being proactive, instead of reactive.

TIP: If you want to learn more about mind-set and goal setting, visit www.MindsetResetPro.com

Chapter 1

Executive Summary

TOP TEN TAKEAWAYS

1. With the right mind-set, you can overcome almost any obstacle or problem.
2. Your WHY is your strongest motivator for change; it is the reason behind all of your actions and thoughts.
3. A goal without a plan is only a dream!
4. People who have written down their goals earn ten times as much as those who don't have any goals!
5. Get very clear about how you will achieve each individual goal.
6. Your choices are based on questions you ask yourself.
7. Ask yourself questions that will give you an empowered point of view. You will develop an innate ability to look for solutions and not problems.
8. By defining your values, you'll discover what's truly important to you.
9. Get out of your comfort zone!
10. Enlist the help of a mentor or a coach.

SIMPLE ACTION STEPS TO TAKE

- Come up with a NEW Key Question and make it your mantra.
- Write down your top ten personal and top ten business goals.
- Find two easy steps to take action on. TAKE ACTION!
- Find an accountability buddy, mentor, or coach!
- Get out of your comfort zone; do something that scares you every day!
- Start implementing new morning, evening, and weekly rituals.
- Start a gratitude journal.
- Plan out your coming week on a Sunday.

NOTES:

Chapter 2: What Sells?

Introduction

The key to selling anything anywhere, online and offline, is to have a product that people want, when they want it!! Even if your product is the greatest invention to come along in decades, if there is no market or demand for it, it will not sell, no matter how hard you try or how cheap you price it.

Choosing the right product to sell is crucial in an era where everything under the sun has already been put up for sale. The main problem, when it comes to selecting a product, is that entrepreneurs look through a single vantage point, rather than through multiple ones. You need to step into the shoes of people in the target market and determine what they need.

Key Areas of Research

The Internet has made it incredibly easy to access information, and it's a treasure trove of sales data that levels the playing field for everyone. An individual with a laptop today has access to ten times the data that large corporations had only a decade ago. As a matter of fact, today a person in Kenya with a cell phone has access to more information than the president of the United States had fifteen years ago.

Finding the right product is important, but if you start off in the wrong direction, no amount of hard work will help you. At this point, it's about working smarter, rather than working harder. Locating the right product to sell will essentially boil down to the kind of research you do.

In this chapter, you will focus on four key areas to find products that will sell: Niche Markets, Trend Research, Niche Products and Services, Complementary Products or Services, and Current Customer Surveys.

By focusing on these four areas, you will be able to determine whether there is a market for a product or a service and decide whether it is financially worth pursuing. First, you will look at existing products and see how they're doing in the market, determine whether the market still has potential for entry, and decide whether you should invest to combat the existing products' hold on the market.

If you have a novel idea that hasn't been seen before, consider whether the need for this product exists in the market. If there really aren't any products in the same category as yours in the market, you have a higher risk of failure, because you need to create a market for your product and build awareness of it.

The Niche Market

No business—particularly a small one—can be all things to all people. The more narrowly you can define your target market, the better. This process is known as "creating a niche" and is key to success for even the biggest companies. Walmart and Tiffany are both retailers, but they have very different niches: Walmart caters to bargain-minded shoppers, while Tiffany appeals to upscale jewelry consumers.

Finding your niche market is essential for your online sales success.

Finding niche products or trends is one of the easiest and fastest ways to ensure that you will have success in your niche. Piggybacking on the success of other products that are already selling like crazy and then offering a product or a service that complements them is a sure-fire way to have success.
Try to find products that fill the gaps in a certain niche or add functionality to products or services. That way, you eliminate the risk of breaking into a totally new market, because the product already comes with a built-in customer base.

Finding Top Sellers

No matter whether you already have a certain product in mind or you have an idea that you think may sell, the first thing you need to see is if there is a similar product or service already on the market, see if it is selling, and check to see what the interest in it is.

To start out, you will just do a Google search to see what you come up with when you enter keywords for products or services you are thinking about selling. The very first thing you'll see will be lists of sites from around the Web, which you'll need to analyze. If, for example, you search for "blenders," Google will deliver to you a bunch of results and a list of websites: Vitamix, Blendtec, Breville, and so on. All are manufacturers of high-end blenders.

NOTE: When doing your research, you will want to jot down the search results—the names of all of your competitors—on a piece of paper or in a spreadsheet, so that you know who you will be up against and you can see who their target market is. This is crucial to learn for the research you will be doing later.

No matter what keyword you enter, you'll usually get three totally different results for the three Google Search tabs. Doing thorough research on Google not only lets you see what is out there, it also gives you alternative options, which is especially important when you are creating new and unique products.

To optimize your search results further, you simply click on the Google Shopping Tab to receive more filtered results of what is for sale. The Shopping search will deliver results regarding prevalent prices in the market, where these products can be bought, and the customer rating of the products.

It is also a good idea to include another filter in your searches by adding "Best Selling (Your Keyword)" or "Top Selling (Your Keyword)," in order to get even more defined results.

Once you have gotten a better idea of what is on the market by browsing the "Shopping" section of Google, click the Images tab, and you'll be surprised by how different the results are. By searching images on Google, you'll be able to see all of the available designs of the product you're thinking of selling.

Searching the images on Google is especially important when you are launching a brand new product, because many times the results you get on Google Images are so dramatically different from those you get with the regular Google search. You may find that what you thought did not exist already exists and is on the market.

Your very next research stop should be Amazon.com. Amazon is also known as a "Buyer's Search Engine." It is where people usually go and search any time they are ready to buy something. The sheer volume of products available and the multitude of reviews are a gold mine of data for entrepreneurs.

Interestingly enough, Amazon makes it very easy for you to see what the best sellers on its site are. With a few clicks, you can instantly see the best sellers in pretty much any category, so I highly recommend that you start your search by using "(Your Keyword) Best Sellers." Or go to the "Movers and Shakers" page, where you will find sales information regarding the popularity of products in terms of sales, percentages in gains, previous ranking, customer ratings, and so on. See if the category you are thinking of entering is worth your while or not. If it is already popular on Amazon, it probably is worth investing in, because there is most likely a good demand for it already. If not, you will need to do further research to establish whether there is a market for it.

Another strategy is to visit sites such as MerchantWords.com, which offer detailed data reports on what people searched for on Amazon. These reports are great for providing ideas about what people are actually looking for. With a bit of digging and a little creativity, you can gather ideas about products or services.

Once you have done some research on Amazon and Google, you will have a better idea of what is out there. Now you'll want to dig deeper by moving over to one of the most powerful tools available to entrepreneurs: Google Trends.

Researching Trends

Google.com/Trends is amazingly fascinating to explore. With this tool, you will be able to see what people are searching for and what interests they have had in previous years. This data goes back a few years, which means you can view how trends have changed with time and how they have affected products in the market.

To show you an example of how something trends, I'll use the term *juicing*. The trend analysis result on the search is for the keyword *juicing*. (See Fig. 2.1.)

As you can see, it is on a steady upward growth curve. This is exactly what you'd want to see if you were thinking of getting into the juicing market or any market. Not only does Google Trends give you the trend data, it also lets you know where people are searching for those terms and what they are searching for. This provides a really good idea of where and what the market interest is in a product.

When you research a product to sell, it's always crucial to look at how the market is trending. Always try to find a product that is on an upward growth trend, which shows that there is interest in it. A waning or downward slope will indicate that the demand for the product is decreasing and the product is beyond its growth life cycle.

Almost every product or service has a certain life cycle, which consists of the stages a product goes through from the time when it was first thought of until it is finally removed from the market. Not all products reach this final stage. Some continue to grow, and others rise and fall. Older, long-established products eventually become less popular, while, in contrast, the demand for new, more modern goods usually increases quite rapidly after they are launched.

You always want to pick a product or a service that is trending upward. Something that gets a lot of searches online is a product that is on people's minds. Make sure it is not past its growth peak; obviously, you don't want to pick a trend that has reached maturity and has no more growth or that is on a decline, because it would mean that interest in it is waning and that sales of the product are probably on the same downward slope.

Fads move almost immediately into the growth stage of the product life cycle. Some fads possess significant residual markets that keep them around for a while, but even these products move fairly rapidly into and through decline.

Consider the iPod, the iPad, and the iPhone. While music players are still relevant today, not too many people are purchasing an iPod that is dedicated only to listening to music, when now they can access the same facility on their iPhones. Because the product no longer provides them with additional utility, its demand in the market has declined. Conversely, the iPad had been observing an upward trend, and the iPhone beats them all, because it provides a better user experience. See Fig. 2.2.

Where you search for information on how certain products or services are selling will vary according to your product and where your target market will be. If you're selling a digital product such as software or an online course, then you should do some research on ClickBank or Warrior Forum and see which categories are popular. If you're providing a service, you'll be best off researching what people are offering on Craigslist or Angieslist. The search strategy on these sites will be the same as the one I described earlier.

Once you've done your research on what is selling and trending, you'll have a better idea about which niche market you can serve more profitably with your product or service.

Identify the Problem, Solve the Problem, Sell the Solution

This is by far my favorite way of coming up with new products or services to sell. Selling solutions to problems is simple, because there will probably be a willing buyer on the other end. With a bit of research, you can find thousands of products or services that people are having problems with, and by doing a bit more research online, you can find solutions to those problems. It is that simple.

First, you are entering a niche market that is already established. Second, you will end up with raving fan customers, because you actually solved a problem or a need they had.

This is how I was able to create a product that gave me financial freedom. Back in the day, I was able to ride the success wave of the iPod by fixing the problem and piggybacking on the iPod's success.

Best of all, you can do the same. First, look for trends and find products or services that are selling like crazy. Next, look at what people are having problems with or are complaining about in the online reviews on Amazon or on user forums. Then find solutions to the problem.

iPods had screens that were prone to getting scratched, and many people were very unhappy about it. There were cases and skins to protect them, but even with those solutions, the iPods still got scratched.

After identifying the problem, I researched a solution that would solve this problem plaguing the iPod community. On Google, I discovered a plastic polish that worked, and I was then able to market it to the "ultra niche " of people who had scratched iPods and actually cared about it.

Chapter 2

What I really had found was the ideal customer, someone who had bought an expensive product because of its cool looks and who had a "pain point."

Fig. 2.1 Google Trends Juicing
(View full-size image at www.internetsalesmastery.com/book_images.html)

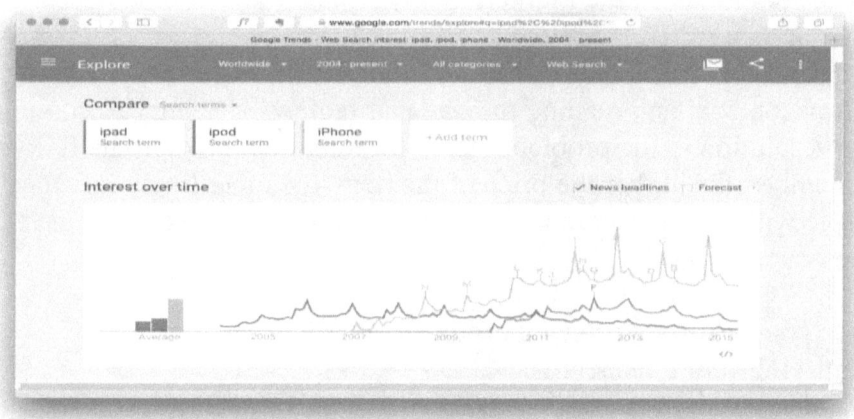

Fig. 2.2 iPod, iPad & iPhoneTrend Chart
(View full-size image at www.internetsalesmastery.com/book_images.html)

Even though I found this niche by pure coincidence, this same formula can be applied to many trends or best-selling products. Many products have flaws or pain points that have not been addressed by the companies selling them because the problem is not on a big-enough scale to impact their sales.

Charger packs for smart phones, smart phone cases, tablet or phone cases and covers, and high-end ear buds are all products that fix shortcomings of products that are already selling well.

Sometimes you don't even have to look too far to identify a problem. It may be best to look for a personal issue you have had or are having with a product or a service and find a solution by doing a bit of research.

Are there any products or services that you currently use and are having problems with? What are the flaws? What can be improved on? What are your friends or your family complaining about? Are there already solutions on the market?

You can spot "pain points" that customers are experiencing by going to Amazon.com and reading the one-star reviews. Then try to come up with a solution to the problem that is prevalent with the product. Remember, the higher the price of the item, the more likely it is that people will buy an accessory or an extra solution to make their user experience better.

Once you have found flawed products, your journey toward identifying solutions begins.

Google and the other search engines are great sources for solutions. With a bit of creative thinking, you will be able to connect all of the dots and come up with a product that solves the problem.

Chapter 2

TIP: *Once you have found a solution, make sure that you are not infringing on copyrights or patents by doing a quick patent search on USPTO.gov. You don't want to invest in a product or an idea that has already been patented, only find out later and get into a legal dispute. If the fix isn't legally protected yet, you can go the extra step by getting a provisional patent for about $250 and start selling the product.*

Survey Your Customers

If you're already selling in the market, then one of the easiest ways to find new products and services is by conducting a survey of the people who buy from you most often and see what they need or want.

You can discover what their challenges or desires are, find solutions and ways to fulfill these, and then market the solutions to them. First, you will be improving your product line and will be serving your customers better, and second, you will show your customers that you care.

TIP: *Even if you don't have a customer base yet, you can gather this information from other sources. If you have a Facebook fan page, survey your fans, or go on niche-specific user groups and online forums and blogs and post questions there. Get to know what people are looking to buy!*

Executive Summary

TOP TEN TAKEAWAYS

1. When doing your research, you will get totally different search results on Google, Google Shopping, and Google Images.
2. Finding your niche market is key to your online sales success.
3. When you're selecting a product to sell, it's always important to look at how the market is trending with Google Trends.
4. Almost every product or service has a life cycle, some longer than others.
5. You always want to pick a product or a service that is trending upward. You obviously do not want to pick a trend on its way down.
6. Fads move almost immediately into the growth stage of the product life cycle, but these products move fairly rapidly into and through decline.
7. Find a problem, solve the problem, sell the solution!
8. Keep an eye on what buyers are complaining about, look for a consistent theme between them, and target a solution to the problem.
9. One of the easiest ways to grow your business is by offering extra products and services to your existing customers.
10. Facebook fan pages or groups are great for conducting surveys, if you do not yet have a customer base.

SIMPLE ACTION STEPS TO TAKE

- Research the names of other companies that sell the same products you are planning to sell.
- Search Google Images and Amazon.com for movers and shakers.
- Look at how items are trending on Google Trends.
- Find a niche market you can serve.
- Identify a problem and find a solution.
- Survey your existing customers or go onto user forums or Facebook and find out what their needs and wants are.

NOTES:

Chapter 3: Know Thy Customer

Before you can start selling anything, you need to know who your customer is going to be.

Identifying your target market will be central to your marketing and sales efforts. It will determine how you engage the customer and how you will persuade the person to make a purchase.

The trick is to identify what customers need and when they will need it and deliver it to them accordingly. But first you need to know who these customers are!

You will have to do more research into who exactly your customers are. You've probably already selected a product or a service you want to offer. Now you want to make sure there is actually a market for your offer, and you also want to know the customers who already buying this product.

The Internet is a gold mine of demographic information. You are going to mine that data to find out exactly who your target customer is, in such incredible detail that it would have been hard to imagine only a few years ago.

In this chapter, you will learn how to identify your target market by studying the demographic data you find online. Then you will create your ideal customer avatar, so that you can laser-target your marketing to that one person you have in mind.

Identifying Your Customer: The Research Phase

Whenever you get into a new market, it's important to do as much research as possible. The more time you spend researching who your target market really is, the easier it will be for you to sell to that specific market.

Search engines and social media sites will become your new best friends in this research process.

Google

I always like to start off my target market research by gauging who the competitors in the field are. By using Google, you can gain a broad view of the market you plan to enter and what else is in that market, as well as who offers the same or similar products or services.

At this point, you should already have an idea about the product or the service you're going to offer. The more information you can gain about who is out there, the better. Normally, I start out Googling the broadest search terms of the product or the service I plan to offer and then get more specific as I go. First, I start by searching for the names of competitors' websites, magazines, or blogs related to the subject, user discussion forums, industry associations, charities, federations, foundations, clubs, societies, and so on—basically, anything that relates to the product or the service I plan to offer. The more data I can collect during this phase, the better.

As I mentioned earlier, while you're doing research it's essential to be very systematic and organized. It is a good practice to input all of the important search results into a spreadsheet, so that later you can easily access the information you gathered.

Once you have collected enough product information on Google and Amazon, you will move on to the next phase of your target market research, which is to gather the exact demographic information of the target market for the product you have selected.

Social media has exploded in the last few years, and the demographic data that these companies have been gathering and offer to their advertisers is second to none, in determining exactly who the target market or customer is. So now you will use the data you collected earlier on Google to dive deeper into locating your target market.

Facebook

Facebook offers one of the best demographic research tools: Facebook Audience Insights. It is available inside the Facebook Ads Manager. If you do not have a Facebook advertising account, you need to sign up right now!

http://.facebook.com/ads/audience_insights/

Facebook Audience Insights lets you see exactly who your target market audiences are, simply by inputting the keywords of companies or product names that you got from your research on Google earlier, in the "Interests" field. Facebook will compile all of the demographic information. See Fig. 3.1.

You will see exactly what percentage of the Facebook population has liked the Facebook pages of those companies, sorted by gender, pages liked, and where the people live, all the way to their household income levels, the value of the houses they live in, and their spending habits. The more interests you add to the search, the more targeted your information becomes, and the better idea you will have about exactly who your customer is.

So, for example, if you were thinking of marketing surf clothes to surfers, you would start out by entering a few of the different manufacturers of surf wear into the interest fields, such as Billabong, Quicksilver, and Oakley. Then you would add a few pro surfers, such as Kelly Slater and Taj Burrow, and maybe a few surf movies, such as *The Endless Summer* (all of these interests were found on Google by searching for [your keyword] products or (top [your keyword] movies).

You end up with a target market demographic of 57 percent women and 43 percent men between the ages of eighteen and twenty-four, who mainly live in Huntington Beach and Honolulu, Hawaii; who surf the Internet from mobile and desktop devices; whose median household income is $50K to $75K; and who live in houses valued at $250K. In addition, 69 percent of these people buy clothing online.

Not bad data, from a site that most people thought was only good for wasting time and posting selfies and pictures of food and cars and of days frolicking on the beach.

If you have not already, before you do anything else online, I recommend that you set up a Facebook fan page and an FB advertising account for your company or product. That way, you'll be able to see exactly what demographic is interacting with and liking your company's page, and you'll get an even more accurate representation

Chapter 3

of who your clients are. The higher the number of fans you get, the more accurate the representation of your potential market will be.

This information can be used in multiple ways and will become especially important when you create Facebook Ad Campaigns and put together your marketing messages, which will be used to drive actual sales in the later stages.

TIP: *By going to the "Page Likes" tab in the Audience Insights tool, you can see what pages the people like, related to the interest. By adding these pages to your "interest," you can further laser-focus in on your exact demographics for your product or service.*

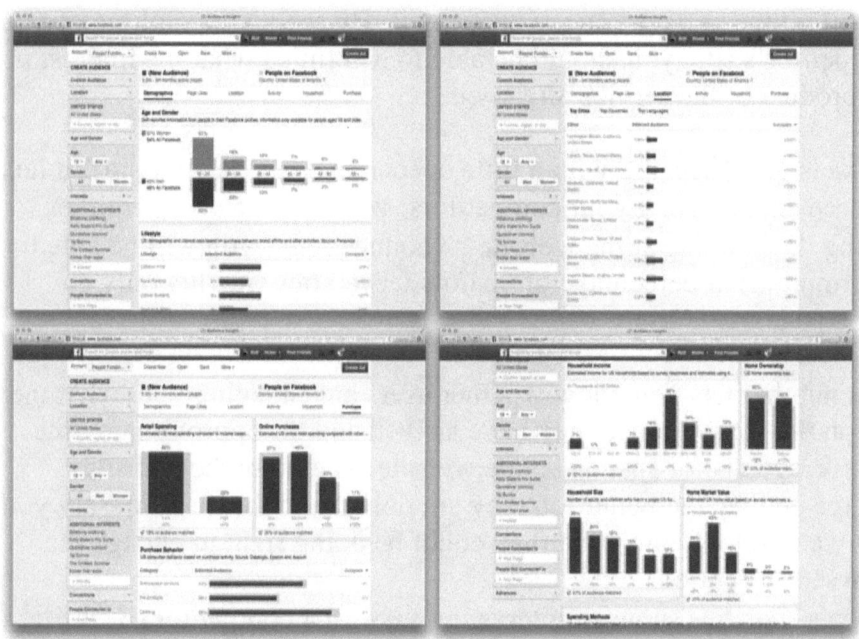

Fig. 3.1 Facebook Audience Insights Charts
(View full-size images at www.internetsalesmastery.com/book_images.html)

Alexa.com

Once you have done your research on Google and Facebook, you will move on to Alexa.com, a Web analytics site owned by Amazon that keeps track of almost every website on the Internet and provides important demographic data on specific websites. This way, you will be able to see exactly who is visiting your competition's website and further pinpoint who your future customer will be.

The very first statistic Alexa gives you is the global ranking of the website you are researching. Although this may not mean much to you right away, the smaller the number is, the more important the site is, and the more interest there is. This will let you determine how important the market you are entering is. By seeing the ranking of your competitor's site, you should be able to determine what the interest in the product or the service already is.

Alexa is great because with a little deeper analysis on your side, it lets you see exactly what your competitors' websites are doing right or wrong. By looking at the website's "bounce rate," you will be able to determine what percentage of visitors leave after viewing only the home page.

This number lets you know whether users are engaging with what they see on the website once they have arrived and the approximate time the average visitor spends on the website. The more the websites engage people, the better job they are doing, and the more closely you will want to look into what they could be doing right to engage the browsers' attention.
Alexa's statistics show an interesting view of a competitor's website, something you would never get by simply visiting a website itself. You will also be able to see the demographics, and you can even learn whether the visitors have children.

This in-depth research would traditionally take months or even years to collect, and it's now right in front of you with the click of a button. The guessing game is over! By studying the statistics, you will be able to gather a complete picture of who the target market is for any given product.

This information is a treasure trove to those who started off with nothing but speculations in the initial stages. The quest, however, does not quite end here, because you need to put all of this information to use. This data will determine a number of decisions that will extend much further than merely identifying your target market, because you will want to use it when you set up your website.

Comparative Analysis

It is very important to take into account the data of a few different websites and social media sources such as Facebook, to get a more accurate picture of what the total rankings are for a particular category.

This is where you will start searching the statistics on Alexa for other websites you have come up with and will compare them to one another, to arrive at a more accurate picture of the exact demographics for your product or service.

Once you've gauged the online standing of several sites, you can compare them against one another to see which demographics stand out the most and what the similarities are in the data you input into your spreadsheet. You need to pay special attention to who is already buying the product or the service you want to sell; then you can align your marketing and sales message toward these people.

Once you have researched the target market of your competition on Facebook and Alexa, you will be able to target the same customer demographic that is visiting your most successful competitor's website, instead of wasting money by marketing to the incorrect demographic. Marketing to the correct demographic makes it more likely that the person will be interested in your product or service. Laser-targeting your demographics is the key to any marketing strategy. The more you know about your customer; the more targeted and therefore effective your message can be.

Your Customer Avatar

Now that you have all of the demographic information in hand about your customer, you can start creating an image of that person, but you are going to take it a few steps further, by creating your own dream customer avatar.

It's very important not to let this future customer remain a vague notion, simply based on numbers, but rather to turn various aspects into reality by creating a real vision of the customer. That way, you'll be able to craft the perfect marketing message that will engage and resonate with people, that will lead them to the sale.

Creating Your Dream Customer Avatar

The best way to sell to a person is by knowing every single detail about him or her. Because you now have a demographic outline of whom your competitors are selling to, you can create a picture of the one person who embodies your dream customer.
You will create your customer avatar from scratch. By now, you know the person's age, gender, income level, and education level from the research you just did. Next, you are going to fill in the blanks and write down every aspect you can account for.

The ultimate aim of this exercise is to have a single person to speak to in your marketing message, so that you can connect in a way that will appeal to him or her most effectively.

To create your customer avatar, you will start by giving your avatar a name, and then you will add facets to the life of your avatar by asking yourself some questions that you will answer by using the demographic data we gathered earlier.

What gender is the person? Where does he or she live? Is the avatar married or single? What education level does the individual have?

Now envision the life of your dream client. What kind of house is the person living in? Will it be a picket fence home or is it an apartment? How big is it? Does the avatar have children or not? If so, how old are they? What school do they go to? What does your avatar do with his or her free time? Does the avatar play golf or football? Go to the gym? Or does he or she not care about staying fit?

This exercise can be as extensive as you wish, depending on how much you want to know about your ideal customer. The deeper you get into the details of your avatar's life, the easier it will become to craft your marketing messages toward that single person. Each and every detail can be planned out, according to the statistics you gathered. Every detail that you find in your research will contribute to the overall success of your message.

Your ultimate goal with this exercise is to understand the needs and wants of your dream customer, allowing you to then deliver custom marketing messages that will resonate with the person.

Once the details have been set, start creating a lifestyle. This data will be important if you want to know how your product or service will fit in with the lifestyle of your customer. To learn about the customer's lifestyle, you can consider the following questions:

What kind of car does the person drive? What does the customer do on weekends? What kind of friends does he or she have? Does the customer go to the gym? What brands of products does the person buy? What books does he or she read? What movies does the customer watch? Whom does the person look up to? What words are more commonly used in his or her vocabulary? Is the customer religious? (If yes, what religion does he or she practice?) Is the customer formal or informal in behavior? What keeps him or her up at night? What is the person's greatest fear?

Write down as many details as you can, and the picture of your dream customer will become very clear. The more you know about the customer you want to attract, the easier it will be to address this person.

The Trader Joe's Customer Avatar

Trader Joe's describes its target customer as an "Unemployed college professor who drives a very, very used Volvo." The image is a simplification, obviously—at any given moment, there are probably zero of these "target customers" in Trader Joe's.

What the "unemployed college professor" image does for Trader Joe's is this: it ensures that everyone in the organization has a common picture of the customer. A crucial element of every strategy is deciding which markets and customers the company will serve. The "unemployed college professor" speaks directly to this issue.

Trader Joe's could have referred to its customers as "people who are of high socioeconomic status and quality-conscious but also budget-conscious, and who value new experiences." Yet this adjective-filled statement doesn't provide as clear an image as the unemployed college professor. Would a professor like the red-pepper soup? Yes, indeed!

Other Ways to Find Your Ideal Customer Avatar

Another way of approaching the subject is to look closer to home. If you already have a customer who is your dream customer, answer all of those questions about this person.

In fact, sometimes you can take a step even closer to home by using yourself as your target customer, if you are the perfect audience for your product. If you fall into this category, then it will be much easier to envision and deliver the right kind of message, because you will know what resonates with you.

Why Have an Avatar?

The need for an avatar arises from the habit that many marketers have, of tending to forget who they're marketing to and ignoring the many aspects governing the customer's life and purchasing decisions. Even if marketers start off with the correct information, it's easy for them to fall off the track. An avatar will help keep all of your messages aligned with the customer's primary motives.

When you know someone, it's much easier to persuade the person. Investing time in creating your dream customer avatar solidifies your ability to persuade. By creating an avatar, you will have someone to direct your message toward, rather than a vague faceless group of people. Through this method, you can tailor your marketing story to the customer's needs and will be able to enter a conversation that is already occurring in your customer's mind.

From this point on, all marketing decisions and messages will revolve around this single person. All offerings will be tailored to the needs, dreams, fears, and desires of this single person. That includes the marketing message, the website, the colors used in your designs, the design of the site, the headlines, and all forms of advertising that you do.

Your customer avatar will be the key to your success. So go ahead and create as many details as you can, and come up with your perfect customer avatar!

Chapter 3

Executive Summary

TOP TEN TAKAWAYS

1. Before you can start selling anything, you need to know who your customer is going to be.
2. Always start off your target market research by gauging who the competitors in the field are.
3. Facebook offers one of the best demographic research tools: Facebook Audience Insights.
4. Alexa.com, a Web analytics site owned by Amazon that keeps track of almost every website on the Internet and provides important demographic data on specific websites .
5. The more you know about the customer you want to attract, the easier it will be to address this person.
6. Another way of approaching the subject is to look closer to home. If you already have a customer who is your dream customer, answer all of those questions about this person.
7. All offerings will be tailored to the needs, dreams, fears, and desires of this single person.
8. Find a problem, solve a problem, sell the solution!
9. Keep an eye on what buyers are complaining about; look for a consistent theme between them, and target a solution to the problem.
10. Sometimes you can take a step even closer to home by using yourself as your target customer, if you are the perfect audience for your product

SIMPLE ACTION STEPS TO TAKE

- Identify your target customer by using Facebook Audience Insights and Alexa.com.
- Create your own "dream customer avatar."
- Check to see how the product you might sell is trending.
- Research negative reviews and find solutions to problems people are having with products.
- Survey your customers.

NOTES:

Chapter 4: Testing the Waters

Will It Sell?

Once you've decided on a product or a service you want to sell online, you'll want to test the waters before you sink all of your efforts into building your website, creating a marketing message, and/or spending capital by purchasing stock or fully developing the product or the service.

To establish whether there is a market for your product or service, you should start test-selling on some of the established sales venues, such as Amazon, eBay, ClickBank, or Elance, which already have a customer base of millions of people.

The most important reason for using third-party sales platforms is to reduce your risk of failure by keeping your startup costs to as close to zero as possible. Other benefits are instant access to a customer base of millions of people who are searching to buy products similar to yours, and the ease and speed of setting up shop on these sites.

The key to successful test-selling is to offer your product or service on a sales venue that matches your customers' demographic and niche as closely as possible. Your product will not sell well, no matter how hard you try, on a platform that does not match your product's niche.

In this chapter, I'll go over all of the main sales platforms that exist and give you some basic tips on setup, sales, and customer service to ensure your success.

There are many established sales platforms to help you in your quest to establish whether a market exists for your product or service. The following is a quick overview of the best places to start test-selling your offerings, so that you can establish which one is best suited for your product or service.

Amazon

Amazon is the largest and best place to offer name-brand products, complementary products and books, and e-books. Amazon is quite often the primary shopping site of choice because of its huge inventory of products. Nearly everything you can imagine is sold here.

Benefits for the seller include an easy, straightforward sales page setup and immediate access to millions of customers worldwide. Amazon can also handle everything from your billing to fulfillment.

Amazon is best for selling books, e-books, name-brand products, complementary products, electronics and accessories, fashion and accessories, home decor, and health and beauty supplements.

eBay

There's a common misconception that eBay is only good for used products and auctions. This is far from true; there are hundreds of thousands of brand-new products being sold outright that bypass the auction model entirely.

People mainly come to eBay hunting for a bargain, and its search results give your product a very different exposure to a totally different group of buyers than Amazon would.

eBay is best for selling name-brand products, complementary products, electronics and accessories, fashion and accessories, home decor, health and beauty supplements, and automotive products.

Etsy and Quirky

Etsy and Quirky have filled a niche for one-of-a-kind, handmade, original, and unique fashion and home decor items. If your item falls into any of these categories, then you should test-sell it on one or both of these platforms to gauge the market response to your products.

Both of these sites are best for selling one-of-a-kind items, fashion and accessories, artsy items, home decor, and health and beauty supplements.

ClickBank, WarriorForum, and Udemy

If you plan to teach online, have an information product, or are planning to sell software, then ClickBank, WarriorForum, and Udemy are your best bet in order to test the waters. Online education is all the rage these days, and rightfully so. There are also platforms like Coursera and Grovo that are less known but are worth a try.

If you produce video training and aren't taking advantage of these platforms, you could be missing out on a great source of income.

These sites are the best if you are teaching or are selling information products, online courses, webinars, and software.

Indiegogo and Kickstarter Crowdfunding

Test-selling products that are brand new to the market or still in the development stage can be a very tricky proposition indeed. First of all, selling something that does not yet exist can get you into a lot of legal trouble. Yet luckily, now there is a solution for this. If your product is still in its initial stages of product development or you require funding for a project or a new idea, then Kickstarter.com and Indiegogo.com are the two platforms where you can establish whether there is a market for your product or service and, better yet, even get them funded at the same time. It does not get much better than that!

What's great about these sites is they don't even require you to have a tangible product for you to be able to market it. By creating a digital version of the product, which you can easily accomplish by using an AutoCAD software or Photoshop, you are ready. This keeps your startup costs to a minimum.

Crowdfunding is best suited for new products, products in the development stage, tech items, online courses, projects, art, video, music, and film funding.

TeeSpring, CustomInk, Skreened, Gearbubble

If you're looking to get into selling T-shirts, mugs, phone cases, or similar items, then these sites are where you'll want to begin. Your startup cost is $0. Best of all, they do it all for you: the production of the shirts, the billing, and the shipping! All you have to do is design your T-shirt, mug, or case, find a market, and promote your product. The manufacturing, sales, and shipping and handling process are all handled by these companies. It is as easy as it gets!

Best for selling T-shirts, mugs, phone cases, etc.

Clarity, Craigslist, Angieslist, and Upwork

Testing and establishing whether there is a market for a professional or freelance services is a bit tougher than testing for physical products. If you're offering a service in a local vicinity, then the best place to start advertising your offerings is on Craigslist.com or Angieslist.com, which give you the opportunity for narrower targeting.

No matter what type of freelance service you offer, Upwork and Elance are freelance service sites, where you can connect with prospective customers who need your business services.

For consulting and business advice, Clarity offers a perfect test platform.

Alternatively, you can also do some laser-targeted local area advertising on Google or Facebook to a certain geographical area at very little cost.

They are best for selling services.

Chapter 4

The Sales Process

Once you have found the sales venue that best matches your offerings, it's time to start selling. You may have to purchase a few sample products from your suppliers or source them at wholesale distributor sites such as Alibaba.com, Alidirect.com, eBay.com, or even Amazon, or you may have found a supplier that will be able to drop-ship the products you plan to sell.

The ultimate motive behind test-selling isn't to make a huge profit immediately, but to keep your startup expenses way down to minimize the initial investment risk of money and time, in order to gauge the viability of the market for the product or the service you want to sell.

Harnessing the power of these established marketplaces will let you reach out to an already-existing target market and will save you a lot of setup time, money, complications, frustration, and guessing.

 Although you don't have an entire website setup to contend with, you still have your product sales page to consider. Setup procedures on most of these platforms are simple and so straightforward that even a total novice without any previous experience can be selling in less than an hour.

The biggest benefit, however, is immediate access to millions of customers as soon as your product page goes live, once you click the "submit" button. Not only will you be reaching out to a large audience, you will be targeting an audience that comes to these sites with the sole purpose of purchasing products or services similar to yours.

You can also bank on the credibility and trust that these sites have already established, without the need to go through the entire process of creating a brand, generating awareness, and building trust, which you would have had to do if you chose to create your own Web sales platform.

Setup

The setup procedures vary a bit from site to site, but all are very simple and straightforward, so that anyone—even someone with the most basic technical knowledge—can have his or her products listed on any of the major sites in less than half an hour.

TIP: *If you haven't had any previous experience at setting up sales pages on a particular site, then it's best to see if the site has a setup helper and follow any tutorial videos that it offers (or search for videos on YouTube) and take good notes. While this may take some time, it is well worth the extra effort, because it will save you endless hours and a lot of frustration during the setup process, and it will give you a good foundation of knowledge about what is and isn't possible on the various sites.*

Writing Item Descriptions

When writing product descriptions, you need to be crystal clear. Your description should detail each and every aspect of your product and what it would entail at the time of delivery. Because there is no tangible product to analyze in an online marketplace, you need to give the potential customer an idea of exactly what to expect once the purchase has been made.

While you want to describe the various aspects of your product in detail, it is important to state very clearly and accurately what your product or service will do or won't do. Do not overstate or over promise what you can't deliver! Going overboard with details may have a detrimental effect.

Rely on images and graphics to deliver information as much as possible, and make sure that the photographs you use are of professional quality: clear, in focus, and on a simple, clean white background.

As with any marketing, your headlines are key to the success of your sales message. Focus on creating attention-grabbing headlines and lines of copy that will engage the customer. (We will go into much greater detail about headlines and copy writing in the following chapters.)
 Also make sure that you master the art of keyword SEO in your headlines and copy, so that your product shows up immediately when a customer searches for it in the search bar.

Using terms such as "Brand New," "Original," "One of a Kind," "The Best," and "Finally, a Solution!" will make your product stand out and will engage your prospect.

Post-Sales and Customer Service

Most people believe that once an item has sold, the sale is done and their job is over. The truth is that once you have sold something, your part of the deal is just starting!

First, make sure that you package your product properly and ship through a reliable service that allows the order to be tracked. Use a speedy delivery service, and always try to upgrade your shipping to the fastest shipping method, because customers love to receive their items as soon as possible. We live in a world of instant gratification; customers love speedy delivery!

Be sure to make it easy for your customers to be able to contact you. Have a dedicated customer service email address, or get a second phone number so that your customers can call you. Be sure to fill out your "seller information" profile page on the sales platform site.

Answer any questions that customers have as soon as possible. This will show that you are professional and will add a personal touch that shoppers love.

Set up systems so that you get in touch with the customers twenty-four hours after they have received their product or service, and make sure that they received what they expected. Following up with your customers right after the sale is an extremely important step, it will not only show your customer that you care and are professional, but it can also prevent many problems, such as bad reviews and returns.

It is said that a happy customer will recommend your product or service to four people, and that an unhappy customer will tell at least twelve. So it pays to keep your customers happy.

If a problem arises, be sure to take care of it immediately and always try to satisfy your customers. If you are unable to resolve the problem, offer a refund ASAP. Do not waste your time and effort or your customer's, trying to make right what can't be made right. Always offer the customer the best resolution and customer experience possible. Offer free returns and solid guarantees, and stick by them. Unhappy customers who have a problem handled quickly and effectively end up being more loyal than if they had never had a problem at all.

Read all of the feedback that you get, and fix any problems and complaints that show up. Improve and fix them so that they do not occur again in the future. The worst thing that can happen is to receive bad reviews about your product, which could lead to a black mark on your reputation and will have a negative effect on your sales.

Make your customer feedback part of your survey, and gauge the responses to measure the success or failure of your product. Also be sure to ask your happy customers to leave reviews and positive feedback for your products on the websites and social media.

Customer service is an integral part of the test sales phase.

Don't Fall in Love!

If your item has not taken off at the speedy success rate you expected, double-check every aspect to see whether your bases are covered. Chances are, you missed out on some crucial areas in the research phase or during the page setup phase, so it's time to go into "diagnostics mode."

There's one easy way to gauge whether the problem lies with your sales technique or with the product or the service itself. Find out if other companies out there are selling the same product or service that you are; if they are successful, the problem lies with you and the way you are selling it, NOT the product or the service!

First off, if you have no sales, make sure everything is working and that you have everything set up correctly, from the sales page to your email links. Check the stats: did anybody click on your offer? If all of this checks out correctly, it's time to dig deeper. It may be your offering or the way you presented your sales message. Is your headline descriptive and does it have impact? Is your sales message compelling? Is it crafted to reach the demographic of your product or service? Does it explain the benefits? Does it speak to the wants, needs, and desires of your customer? Most important, does the market really want this product?

After you check to see that you covered all of the bases, have made all of the necessary changes, and have tried several variations many times, and you still are not getting any sales, SWITCH PRODUCTS!! Don't fall in love with your idea or product, even though you think it is the best product out there. It just may not be!

Too often, entrepreneurs fall in love with their product or service and forget that it is the customer's needs, not their own, that they must satisfy. Step back from your daily operations and carefully scrutinize what your customers want. Suppose you own an online pet store. Sure, customers come to your online pet store for cat food, but is food all they want? What could make them come back again and again and ignore your competition? The answer might be quality, convenience, reliability, fun, ease of browsing, or customer service.

Your product idea could be revolutionary, a breathtaking total game changer. Yet none of that matters if no one will buy it. Being a successful entrepreneur means being a competent entrepreneur; know when to kill an idea and go on to the next!

Chapter 4

Executive Summary

TOP TEN TAKEAWAYS

1. To establish whether there is a market for your product, test-sell on Amazon, eBay, Overstock, and so on.
2. Sell on the third-party sales venue that best matches your product or service.
3. When writing product descriptions, you need to be crystal clear. Although you want to describe the various aspects of your product in detail, it's important to practice moderation and not to overstate or overpromise.
4. Your headlines are key to the success of your sales message.
5. Once an item has sold, your part of the deal is just starting!
6. Whenever possible, upgrade your client's order to the fastest shipping method, because customers love to receive their items as soon as possible. We live in a world of instant gratification!
7. Make it easy for your customers to contact you.
8. Set up systems so that you get in touch with customers twenty-four hours after they have received their product or service, to make sure that they received exactly what they expected.
9. Don't fall in love with your idea or product, even though you think it is the best product out there. It just may not be.
10. Other companies out there are selling the same product or service that you are; if they are successful, the problem lies with you and the way you are selling it, NOT with the product or the service.

SIMPLE ACTION STEPS TO TAKE

- Pick one or two of the established sales websites that match your product's niche.
- Write clear and precise product descriptions and use good-quality photos to supplement the description.
- Answer all customers' questions ASAP!
- Upgrade shipping to a speedier service for faster delivery.
- Follow up with your customers once the orders have been received to make sure all is as they expected.
- Ask for reviews and feedback.

NOTES:

Chapter 5: Setting Up Your Online Presence

Once you have had some success selling your product or service on one or two of the established sales platforms and have determined that there is a market for your offering, it's time to set up your own online sales platform, to further grow sales and establish your brand and your online presence.

Your website is probably the first real contact your prospects will have with you or your product, so it's critical that you get it right.

An online presence is crucial to any brand, product, or service today. Creating an online presence from scratch, however, requires carrying out certain steps with attention to detail. The key steps to creating a great online presence are once again based on the research data you gathered about your target market, and everything you do on your site is designed to serve your customer avatar.

In this chapter you will select a domain name, set up the website hosting, design and build the site and your shopping platform, set up payment systems and email auto responders, and finally test everything to make sure you are ready to go live with your own site

The Pre-Build

Once again, you will go back to do some final research on competitors' sites on the Internet. This step, however, will not be as taxing as the previous phases. You have done the mammoth share of research, which amounts to about 80 percent of the required information that you need to build a successful site.

By having your target customer, you know who you will be marketing to, which makes the process of tailoring your online presence to this person easier.

The research notes that you've gathered so far should include competitors' names and websites, a list of keywords derived from the Google keyword tool that are related to your product or niche, and all of the demographics of the customers you are targeting.

The most important part of the data you will use in designing your website will be the demographic information you compiled thus far, because you want to focus on building your website to suit your target market and your customer avatar as much as possible.

Now that you have this information, you will delve into analyzing what your competitors are doing right and wrong and focus on the design they've implemented on their sites. You'll be studying everything, from the images they used to the content they're sharing, all the way down to the colors on their sites, while you also keep a close eye on the headlines and calls to actions they use.

To give you a good idea of what to be on the lookout for, let's study a totally niche item for your website research . . . high-powered, high-priced blenders! This niche has really been trending like crazy lately, and you'll get a very good idea of what to look out for when you analyze your competitors' sites, in order to see what works and what does not. In this case, you'll start off at the website of Vitamix, makers of a super-expensive, high-speed blender. See Fig. 5.1.

What's great about Vitamix's site are the clarity and minimalism in the site design, where you know immediately what the site is all about. In fact, there is a whole lot more you can tell about Vitamix by just looking at the front page of its site.

No matter what successful website you look at, they always have three things in common: simplicity of design, ease of navigation, and focus on the target market.

Apple, Google, Amazon, and every other successful site online are uncluttered, straight to the point, and easy to navigate. When you visit the Vitamix page, you are in no doubt of what the company is selling or what the site is about. The clean page and the smart use of images immediately inform you what Vitamix is selling: blenders and cooking. There is no question about it!

When you design your site, it's important that everything on your main page conveys to the visitor what your website is about or what you are selling. The first thing you see on the Vitamix site is a model dressed in a purple sweater, happily greeting visitors to the site. She represents the exact customer demographic of Vitamix, and she is showing the product in an environment where it would normally be found, in a beautiful upscale home, just as the demographics that we compiled earlier reflect.

Navigation on the site is extremely easy, and no time is wasted in searching. Ease of navigation is extremely important, because as soon as you make it too complex and users can't quickly find what they're looking for, they will most likely abandon the site for another one, or go back to Google to search for a site that delivers what they need.

It is vital that your site provides access to important information that the browser is seeking in the fastest, most convenient way possible. Think about the simplicity of Google's search page . . . it has only the name of the company and the search field. On Apple's site, the clarity of the navigation lets you find what you want in a matter of seconds. There should never be any guessing about anything on your site; simplicity is key in order to cut distraction and ease navigation.

Vitamix has taken a leaf out of this book; it delivers a structured site that is easy on the eyes and is simple to use. The ease of use and the clarity of design on Vitamix's site are major contributing factors to its success, which you saw when looking at the Alexa data. Vitamix has low bounce rates and longer engagement times than Blendtec, because Vitamix follows these simple rules.

Before we look further at the website, though, let's just refresh our memory on Vitamix's demographics by using the Facebook Audience Insights page and typing *Vitamix* into the interests section.

The results we come up with reveal that most women engaging with Vitamix are married women ages thirty-five to fifty-four with a college degree, who make more than $75K a year, and who live in houses valued at more than $500K. When we look at everything about the design of the Vitamix site, it is 100 percent congruent with, and reflective of, those demographics.

Consider what your website is working toward. The ultimate aim of a Web page should always be evident. This site is completely geared

Chapter 5

toward one mission: cooking. Everything is obviously targeted toward women ages thirty-five to fifty-four, who live in nice homes. This is evident from the women featured in the site's photographs.

I would also like to point out that Vitamix does some subtle little things that make very big differences. Vitamix doesn't yell out its call to actions; this would not sit well with the company's demographic. But Vitamix uses them in a very smart way, by making its Products tab a call to action and calling it "Shop Products." It is just a single click away, without overselling the product. It is also the very first tab on the website links. Very sneaky and very clever.

Remember that the website should provide information and value. The user's visit here should be made worthwhile with added information that a visitor would like to see. In Vitamix's case, it has incorporated recipes into its page. This was done in an effort to keep customers on the site for a longer period of time, and to offer the browser as much useful information about the product and the use of the product as possible, in order to build rapport and trust.

The more value customers receive from the site, the greater the chances that they'll make a purchase. Create a list of objectives you want to achieve with your website and how you can add value to people visiting it. Consider what value your website can provide to visitors that they won't get on other sites and that will engage them to stay on your site longer.

Another thing that's interesting is the manner in which Vitamix markets to two different target markets from within one site. You will notice that in the top menu bar, you have the option of selecting between "for home" or "for business" Web pages. If you look at the two pages, you'll notice that everything on them is totally different, except for the product they sell.

The two pages in Fig. 5.2 show just how different the marketing methods are within the same site. The business page on the left stresses the importance of the product for bars and restaurants. The image shows a bar setup, demonstrating the product used in a professional setting, and the model exactly matches the target audience Vitamix is selling to.

The image in Fig. 5.2 on the right is taken from the "Home" section, where a recipe page is featured. The image also focuses on food placed on a traditional dining table. The differences between the two sites occur in the links used, the resources provided, the performance, the product, and the purchase methods. Three important aspects are the differences in the colors, images, and text that are used.

The copy on the business page also offers very different value to the user, keeping the professional in mind. It describes business success stories, best practices, and bonus business trips. Are you going to be catering to a business market or to the home end user or both? How can you separate your messages?

It is always a good idea to research several websites to get the best ideas about what is working or not. For our next step, you will visit another blender company's website, Blendtec, and see what kind of content it has added to its site. The different marketing strategies of the two sites are immediately evident. The images on the Blendtec site don't attract the eye and aren't as engaging as Vitamix's.

There is no immediate view of value being provided on this site, and the images feature only a blender. While it does fulfill the aim of conveying that the site is for blenders, it does little else. The site itself does nothing to capture the interest of the reader and entice her to stay there for a longer period. Blendtec's site is not as personal and targeted as Vitamix's and does not engage the visitor. See Fig. 5.3.

Chapter 5

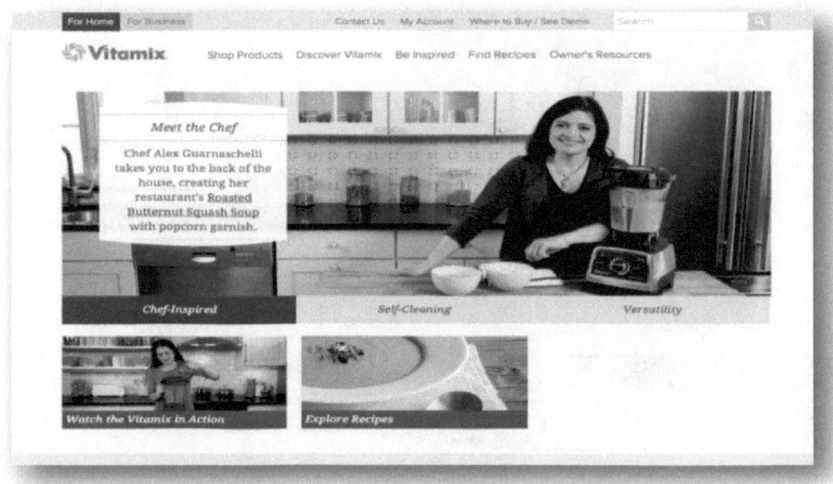

Fig. 5.1 Vitamix.com Home Page
(View full size image at www.internetsalesmastery.com/book_images.html)

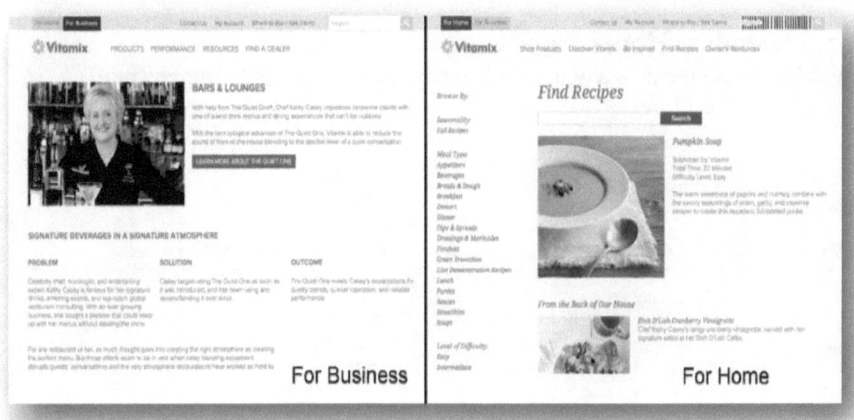

Fig. 5.2 Vitamix.com for Business and for Home
(View full-size images at www.internetsalesmastery.com/book_images.html)

Setting Up Your Online Presence

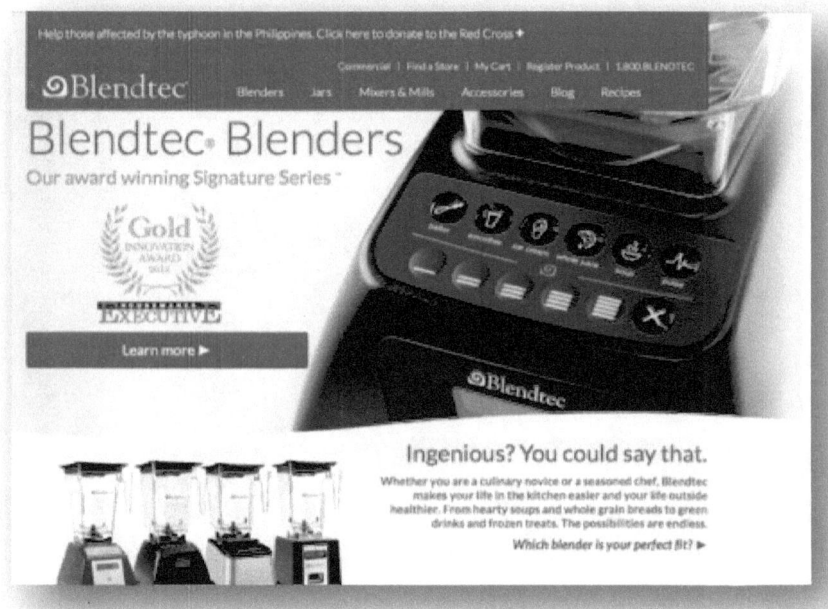

Fig. 5.3 Blendtec Home Page
(View full-size image at www.internetsalesmastery.com/book_images.html)

Engagement Metrics			
Site	Pageviews/User	Bounce Rate	Time on Site (minutes)
blendtec.com	2.96 ▼ -3.90%	49.20% ▲ +7.00%	3:01 ▲ +1.00%
vitamix.com	4.30 ▼ -12.88%	35.40% ▲ +13.00%	3:54 ▼ -12.00%
breville.com	1.10	82.40%	0:26

Fig. 5.4 Alexa.com Bounce Rates
(View full-size image at www.internetsalesmastery.com/book_images.html)

The menu bar at the very top focuses only on the different features and accessories of the blender itself. All of these factors determine whether a user will stay on the site or will add to the bounce rate. The bounce rate reflects whether people stay on the page or go back to browsing other sites after viewing a site's first page.

If you study the Alexa.com results (see Fig. 5.4), you will see the differences between the two websites, in terms of page views and bounce rates. The statistics in this case are rather astonishing. Blendtec has a bounce rate of 50 percent, which means that half of the people coming to the site go no further than the first page before leaving!! This means Vitamix has a better stick rate.

If you take a closer look at how this could be, you'll see that it's partly based on how the sites' designs engage their customers' demographic. Vitamix does it with a direct image of that exact demographic and by immediately engaging the visitor by displaying photos of cooking, along with recipes.

Further on in Chapter 5, we will look into a strategy that Blendtec uses to engage its target market, which is totally innovative and the main reason the company is hugely successful.

What image could you use to engage people directly? Something that would visually explain to your customers what your business is all about when they visit your website? What information could you offer in order to keep them browsing on your site?

Points of Analysis

No matter what site you're analyzing to help you make decisions on your own site design, you need to consider certain factors to make sure that all aspects of the site are covered and that you don't repeat the same mistakes other sites are making.

What demographic are they targeting with their sites? How have they adapted their sites to this demographic? What are their domain names? Do their domain names reflect their brand? How memorable are the names? Are the sites easy to navigate? What links are used throughout the sites? How easily can information be found?

How easy is it to contact the companies? Are they using live chat for their customer service? Do they have an 800 number? Do they have an FAQ page? What are the total number of pages on their sites? What colors are prevalent on the sites? What do the images they use on the sites show? Do the sites have interactive content or videos that engage the visitor to hang out there? Are they offering free reports or samples in exchange for an email address?

Are there testimonials or reviews on the sites? Do the companies have other social proof on their sites, such as magazine articles or news stories?

These questions will help you reach definite answers and gain an in-depth understanding of how all elements within your competitors' sites were used. This information can then serve as a framework for the design of your own site. It will also show you what additional elements you need to work on to stand apart from them.

Testing Your Competitors

To get an even better in-depth view of exactly what your competitors are doing, subscribe to any newsletters they have, email them for more information, use their live chat feature if they have one, and even go so far as to buy their product. Examine their sales sequence to see how they deliver, and look at what can be improved or what parts are missing in their sales process. How is their follow-up? How does their product return policy work? Test everything, model the parts that really work, and improve on the ones that don't.

If you analyze what your competitors say they sell, not only their product or service characteristics, but also the benefits they are selling, you can learn a great deal about how companies distinguish themselves from competitors, and with a bit of creativity you will be able to do the same.

Building Your Web Site

You are finally done with the research phase, and it's time to start designing your website!

Domain Name Selection

Now you are ready to take the first steps toward creating your own website. Before you can set up shop, however, you'll need to buy some digital land. Your domain name is the digital address of your online business, so you must make it memorable and easy on the tongue. One strategy for locating the right fit for your domain name is by visiting the Google AdWords keyword planner tool. It will ensure that the name uses keywords that are easily searchable in the organic rankings. The keyword planning will let you know the search terms most often used by your target market.

The keyword planner allows you to look at the words or the phrases people typically search for on Google. In your domain name, you want to use high-relevance keywords that pertain to your product or service, so that when people search, your domain name shows up higher in the listings. Google's algorithm is constantly changing, so this is less important than it was a few years ago. Yet nevertheless, the more descriptive and popular the keyword you use, the more memorable your domain name will be.

Once you have a list of keywords, you will be ready to head toward domain registration of your site. One of the most popular services in this case is GoDaddy.com, which I personally recommend, as it offers everything you need, but almost any registration company will do domain registration and hosting. Normally, you can be set up and ready with both in less than twenty minutes.

It is good practice to make sure that you completely handle the registration process yourself or, if you outsourced it to a third party, such as the web designer or developer, that you double-check that all emails, billing, and ownership addresses are in your name and not in the name of the web design company, in order to avoid problems down the road.

This step is a security measure, in case you want to switch design or hosting services in the future and you find out that you are not showing up as the owner of your domain name. This way, you won't have to go through the lengthy hassle of getting all of this information transferred to your name later on.
Remember to write down all access passwords and hosting details and keep them in a secure location for future reference.

TIP: *Most companies will offer you for the option of also buying a different version of the same domain, which may end in ".org." Make sure to completely avoid any URLs that end in ".net." If you're doing business in the United States, be sure to use a ".com." Don't bother with any of the others, unless you are an organization.*

Web Hosting

Your hosting site is where your website will be living. You can buy a domain name but may choose to host it on another server. You can simplify your life by using GoDaddy's services to handle all of your domain and hosting needs. Yet almost all registration and hosting services provide cheap, reliable services. There are several listed in the resources section at the end of the book.

Similar to the domain name, make sure to register the hosting in your name, rather than in that of the web designer and his or her company, so that all rights, billing information, and additional information are directed to you.

Design and Build

Now that the technicalities have been taken care of, the real fun begins! During the construction phase, you will have to make many pivotal choices, as you can either go for a custom-made solution for your site or opt for a pre-made commerce solution that will be easy to set up.

I personally recommend that you start off with pre-made solutions, because they are extremely easy to use, and the setup process can be completed by anyone. Very little technical knowledge is required, and the site can be up and running within a day or two.

In addition, you will have a payment system already set up and won't be required to obtain additional services, such as credit card merchant services or shopping cart software. The downside, however, is that your design will be limited by the theme options the service offers, and you get less flexibility for customization.

If you opt for a custom solution, you will need to hire a web designer or a design company to create a site, unless you already have design and website-building knowledge. You will also need to set up a shopping cart solution and payment system. The downsides to this situation are that it will take a considerably longer time (sometimes up to several months) to get online, and it will also be considerably more expensive.

Shopify.com has perhaps the most popular and best e-commerce pre-made solutions available today. The design templates are extremely clean and minimalist and can be adapted to almost any specifications. Conversely, if you want a complete custom site, then basing it on WordPress will be your best bet. WordPress is easy to learn, delivers customizable solutions, and has a plethora of widgets and plug-ins that you can use to do anything you want. Although other solutions, such as Joomla, Wix, and Web Muse, offer the same functionalities, WordPress is often used because of its SEO compatibility and scalability.

If you choose to work with a web designer or a design company on a custom solution, it's a good idea to insist that the designer use WordPress in the creation process. First, because WordPress is extremely customizable through the use of plug-ins. A great e-commerce plug-in is WooPress. The plug-ins are highly adaptable and can be used to easily create a custom website, based on your personal specifications.

As WordPress is a universal and very widely adapted website creation platform, it will allow the replacement of anyone on the team to instantly be up to speed. If your designer selected specific software other than WordPress, you will need to locate someone who will be well versed in the specific software that was used to create the site in the first place.

No matter whether you are using a pre-made service, such as Shopify or Squarespace; or use a site such as Weebly, where you "build" your own site yourself via drag and drop; or if you hire a designer, make sure to choose a clean and minimalist design that will showcase your product well. In addition, make sure that the page is responsive, which means that the content will readjust itself to the display size, regardless of what device people view your site on.

Once again, make sure you are registered as an administrator on the website and that you have complete access to the entire site.

Design

Whether you opt for a custom solution or a pre-made solution, the ultimate aim of your efforts must be the same: pleasing and connecting with your target customer.

You need to keep in mind how your target customer would navigate your site and know what purpose he or she would use it for. Consider what added value you will provide to this person through your website and whether he or she will want to make purchases on the site as a result.

Think about where your target customer will be when browsing your website. Will your customer mainly be viewing your site on a mobile device or at home, in the office or on the road? You can actually find this information by using the Facebook Audience Insights tool. Be sure that your site is mobile ready by using an adaptive design that will make the browsing experience fit perfectly on all devices, because you always want to make the browsing experience a great one.

Once you have customers on your site, what efforts will you make so that they remain there or keep coming back? What marketing strategy will you use? Will you provide additional bonuses, such as newsletters, samples, or freebies?

Colors

Colors play a vital role in the customer's perception. Each color triggers a different emotion in the customer's brain and alters his or her perception of your company. Blue, being the color of trust, is most often used by banks, whereas red denotes excitement. The chart in Fig. 5.5 shows which emotions various colors convey. Consider what emotion you want your target market to feel when visiting your site, and select that color to be the main one featured on your website.

Studies have, in fact, revealed that about 90 percent of on-the-spot decisions are heavily influenced by color.

The use of the right colors, the right division of weight on the Web page, and a clean design contribute to building user trust.

Fig. 5.5 Color Trigger Chart
(View full-size color image at www.internetsalesmastery.com/book_images.html)

Web Design Resources

Design entails much more than simply creating content and placing it on the page. In fact, a number of elements need to be worked on.

Logo Design

If you're looking for a logo design solution that won't cost you much, fiverr.com, 99 Design, Elance, or Upwork are good places to find talented designers who will create great designs to make your brand or product stand out.

Custom Site Design Templates

The site 99designs.com offers custom Web design templates and high-end designs. Designers on the site may even bid on your project, allowing you to select the one that provides you with the most value.

If you opt for a WordPress page, then you can find some affordable theme designs at DIY Themes, Tesla Themes, Theme Forest, or Woo Themes. If you search a bit, you may even be able to locate some for $0.

Images

Images are typically protected by copyrights. This means that you can't just select an image from the Google Image Search to use on your page. In addition, you need to add high-resolution professional images to your website to contribute to the existing theme. There are hundreds of stock photo sites on the Internet that will provide you with royalty-free images. Adobe Stock, Corbis, iStock, or ShutterStock are some great examples of where you can purchase amazing images for low prices and stay out of legal trouble.

eCommerce Store Setup

If you choose not to set up a custom commerce solution, you can make use of many of the tools available on the Internet to set up a shopping cart and a merchant account.

If you're just starting out, 1Shopping Cart is a great solution. In addition, you'll have to set up a PayPal or Stripe account for payment and credit cards or get a merchant account from your local bank or at EmpowerMerchant.com, so that you can start to accept credit cards.

PayPal is a good online payment solution, because it is a very trusted and preferred online payment system for many online shoppers. Many people are still wary of using shopping carts on smaller websites. By offering PayPal as an additional payment method, you will provide extra legitimacy for your site. Having your site verified and approved by VeriSign or Visa also adds an extra layer of trust.

Email Automation

The final but probably most crucial component of your online presence will be your email auto responder. An auto responder service will send out emails automatically to your existing mailing list or when someone signs up for your email list via your opt-in box.

Your auto responder will be the most important component of your marketing strategy and is also the main tool you will be using to establish and maintain customer relations. Once you have set up the auto responder, it will help you not only send out emails automatically but also manage your mailing lists in an effective and automated manner.

The benefits of automated email are perhaps endless. Adding an opt-in on your website will ensure that you can keep on communicating with people who visited your site and joined your mailing list. The email addresses are added to your mailing list automatically, and then you can send people special offers and more valuable information that you scheduled beforehand.

A multitude of email automation solutions are available on the Internet at various prices and with different features. Three that are good to start off with include iContact, GetResponse, and AWeber. The features they offer are very similar; the level of sophistication provided by the email automation services differs, according to how much you're willing to pay for them.
Once you are doing enough business to justify the expense, you can also integrate existing email systems with CRM (customer relationship management) services, such as Sales Force, AWeber, and Infusionsoft or Ontraport.

Yet for starting out, a simple autoresponder service will do just fine, because the learning curve and prices for these more sophisticated solutions are much, much higher.

Testing

Once you have everything set up and feel that it's ready to go, it's time to test your site to see if it really is running as expected. This is a crucial step, because you don't want to be doing damage control once your website has gone live. The last thing you want is for your customers to have problems with your site. Nothing will make customers go elsewhere faster than a buggy site.

Start by going over your copy several times; be on the lookout for typos of any kind, and ensure that all of your prices and item numbers on the checkout cart are accurate, so that you don't have problems when it comes to fulfilling orders.

Check all contact information, email addresses, telephone numbers, and physical addresses for errors. Once you have gone through everything once, go through the test again.

Make sure that all images are loading, and, above all, check that all of the links work. Nothing is more annoying than landing on a 404 error page!

Be sure that the shopping cart is working properly!!

Make sure all of your "thank you" pages are in place, the ones the customer receives after opting in to your mailing list and the ones that should appear after someone buys. Double-check that your email auto responder is delivering the "thank you" and order confirmation emails after someone has ordered.

Test your email auto responder to make sure your messages are being delivered properly, that it is receiving all of the input from the opt-in forms, and that all of the follow-up messages are proofread and are ready to go.

Chapter 5

Executive Summary

TOP TEN TAKEAWAYS

1. The most important part of your research tools that you will use to design your website will be the demographic information.
2. Make sure to register the hosting in your name, rather than in that of the web designer and his or her company, so that all rights, billing information, and additional information are directed to you.
3. Think about how your target customer would navigate your site and what purpose he or she would use it for.
4. Be sure that your site is mobile ready by using an adaptive design that can make the browsing experience great on all devices.
5. No matter whether you are using a pre-made service such as Shopify, Weebly, or Squarespace or hiring a designer, choose a clean, minimalist design that will showcase your product.
6. WordPress is easy to learn, delivers customizable solutions, and has a plethora of widgets and plug-ins that you can use to do anything you want. Base the design of your site on WordPress, even if you are using a web designer or a design company.
7. Ninety percent of on-the-spot decisions are heavily influenced by color.
8. Use only photographs you have taken, or else buy stock images. Do not grab images off the Internet.
9. Email auto responders will be a very important part of your marketing strategy.
10. Testing is a crucial step, since you don't want to be doing damage control once your website has gone live.

SIMPLE ACTION STEPS TO TAKE

- Research your customer demographic information.
- Select a good hosting company and make sure the billing. information, and additional information are directed to you.
- Select a eComerce solution.
- Carefully select the colors you want to use on the triggers color chart.
- Get a email autoresponder.
- Test everything!
- Test everything… again!

NOTES:

Chapter 6: Marketing

By this point, you should be selling your products on your own website, as well as on one or two major established e-commerce sites. Hopefully, you are seeing some good results already.

In this chapter, we will go over everything you need to do to get your message out, from writing copy with a lot of impact to making a compelling offer and learning how to engage your audience with the various social media platforms. Finally, we will look into how to create an email list to build rapport and trust with your prospects so that you can start marketing to them in such a way that they'll end up buying from you.

You now need to shift your focus toward engaging customers on various platforms and driving traffic to your site with your sales message. Successful marketing is all about getting in front of the right audience with the right message at the right time.

Your marketing and sales efforts at this point should be focused entirely on a single target market, and it is on this target market that you will use a laser-focused marketing approach, to convert these people from prospects into customers.

Creating the Sales Message

The average person sees more than 3,800 marketing messages every day; that is 1,387,000 messages every year. Not only are we overwhelmed by the marketing we see, we are bored by the advertising messages we see. How many of these ads do you ever remember or really see on any given day?

The problem is that no matter what business you are in, hundreds or even thousands of others are out there with marketing messages that attempt to get the attention of the very same person you are going after. Most of them are trying to get their messages across by using the "If they don't seem to hear us, we need to talk louder" approach. It really doesn't matter how strong, loud, or long your message is—it's all about how relevant you are to your audience!

If you want to make your business and marketing more memorable, then your marketing needs to tell a story. Story-selling gives your brand context. It tells a narrative of how the product fits into the fabric of your consumers' everyday lives—not just the pretty pictures, but also the honest way people interact with your product. It's weaving your brand into the relevant passion points of your consumer's life.

For your marketing message to work, you will need to craft a unique story that speaks directly to your target market. The more specifically crafted your message is toward your audience, the more chances you will have of eliciting your desired response from them, which is for them to buy your product or service.

To help your prospects arrive at this decision, you need understand the problems they face and position your product as the ultimate solution for them by clearly explaining how your product or service will solve their problems. You need to structure your message so that it elicits answers from them.

Questions that your engagement efforts should answer include: What initial concerns does your customer have? What are your customers looking for? What are your prospects' biggest fears? What are their desires? What do they really want? What problem can your product or service fix?

You want to enter a conversation that is already occurring in the customer's head and build on it. Then after you gain the trust and respect of your prospect, you want to structure your message so that your offer eventually becomes a "Hell, yes!" solution so that the person cannot ignore or refuse to take action on.

For example, if you were a car salesperson, to get this conversation started you could ask yourself what someone who wants to buy new or a used a car may be thinking about. Maybe the person is wondering how much their old car is worth? Are potential customers wondering how they could sell their old vehicle for the most money? Or are they worried about getting the best deal on their new purchase?

You could craft your message by giving them tips on how best to sell their old cars or teach them how to get the lowest price on a new car. You could inform them about the top ten tactics that most car salespeople use to get people to buy a car, thereby establishing trust and differentiating yourself from the competition.

You could create short fun videos and post them on your website and on social media sites, such as Facebook, Twitter, YouTube, or Instagram, or send them directly to your prospects once they have opted in to your email list. (Remember to always include a call to action and a URL at the end of your videos, so that when you post them elsewhere, other than on your site, you drive visitors back to your website!)

The more valuable the information that you deliver to your prospects, the more you will engage them, the sooner they'll trust you, the sooner they will connect with you, and the sooner they will buy from you!

Put yourself in the shoes of your prospects . . . what could your prospects be asking themselves? What are their fears and desires? How will doing business with you benefit them? What information can you offer to benefit your future customers? What can you offer your current customers? What tips can you give them? What can your unique angle be?

It's important to reach out not only to new customers, but also to those who have previously done business with you. People whom you have done business with in the past are a lot more valuable than those who have not, because you already know that they will buy your products!

Once again, using the example of a car salesperson, he could provide his existing customers with maintenance tips on how to avoid costly repairs, tips on how to get the best gas mileage, or safe driving tips. Keep your current customers engaged by delivering helpful information that will educate them and keep building trust, on an ongoing basis.

A customer chooses whether to connect to you or not; people will usually respond only if it's in their best interest. Personal values will ultimately drive their behavior, so ideally you should identify and align with their existing values.

Benefits vs. Features

Always sell the benefits of your product or service, not the features!

There's no doubt about it; most people do not enjoy being sold to and will resist. A customer might know your product or service and may even mentally want to buy it, but the person still might not be moved to action. Buyers will often push back or try to find reasons not to buy your product or service. Their resistance could be as subtle as skepticism, but you must deal with it squarely.

When crafting your sales message, always sell the benefit and always spell out *the benefit of each benefit* (what the benefit will do) and how it will improve your prospect's life.

Each benefit needs to be presented in a crystal-clear way, so that your future customer can identify with it on a deeper personal level. When you present the benefits of the product to the prospects, they will be able to better understand how the product or the service will work in their lives and solve their problem.

Features aren't what entice customers to buy. A benefit answers the question "What's in it for me?" Features aren't effective in engaging the customer and appealing to them. The only time the features might come into play is when a customer is comparing two products in order to make a purchase decision.

The benefits will tackle aspects that will improve the buyer's quality of life. Benefits, in themselves, suggest how buying this product will improve the life of the user. What you want to do is match the benefits your product or service can deliver to the dreams and desires of your target audience.

Think about who they will become by using your products, and include this in your sales message. What benefits will they reap by using your product or service?

Think about the product or the service you're offering. How will it benefit your customers? What desires will it fulfill for them? Make your message as personal as you can, and always use the word *you* when addressing your prospect. Direct your message totally toward this individual or to those the person cares about most. Identify with the customer's problem and offer him or her your solution; be very specific about the details and the benefits of the benefits.

You want your message to appeal to the prospects' identity and to who they are and who they want to become. The more specific you are in your message, the more the person will connect with your message. When writing down benefits, make sure that the benefits you are highlighting will be seen as worthy benefits by your prospects. Try to help them envision owning and using your product and show them exactly how it will improve their lives. Identify the problems that need to be corrected and how your product will help in solving them. If a benefit seems unbelievable or overstated, your customers will become skeptical of your product or claims.

The ultimate goal is to make customers agree with your claims. Help them understand that your product really is what they need. Once they start agreeing with you and start saying yes in their minds, over and over again, to the questions that you use in your sales copy, they will be more likely to make a purchase.

Use your marketing copy to keep soliciting questions that will elicit yes answers from them. The more you can get people to agree with you on small points, the quicker and more likely that they will see how your product or service is a great match for them . . . and the sooner they will buy!

Honing Your Message

The message you deliver to your customer is of paramount importance. Most writing that is designed to persuade either sinks or swims right out of the gate. Whether it's the title of an article or the headline of a sales page, readers make snap decisions based on a quick scan of the top of the page. More often than not, they simply move on to something else, unless you craft an excellent headline. People hate to be sold to but love to buy!

You need to have a strategic focus on what you're going to say to them and how you will deliver it. You will have to tailor and hone your language to your target market. People will not buy your product or service unless they truly understand exactly what you are selling. The perceived value of your product or service will be judged not so much on the item itself, but on how well you present it and are able to communicate its value.

When creating your message, be it for your website, an email campaign, or ads, you need to pay special importance to your headlines, so you must craft them with as much impact as possible.

The Headline

Your headline is by far the most important part of your copy and needs to work like a hook that will reel the customer in. Keep your headline short and to the point. Your headline should spark the reader's attention and curiosity and entice him or her to keep reading your message or take an action. If it does not do this, it is not a good enough headline.

Craft your headline so that it sells the main benefit of your product or service right away. Promise the readers something valuable. Will you teach them how to learn a new skill? Will you unlock a mystery?

Here are some quick, simple examples of what an effective headline looks like:

"25 Ways to Lose 30 Pounds in 30 Days!" "How to Learn French in a Month!" "7 Steps to More Sales!"

There are several ways you can approach structuring your headline. One is by recognizing a problem and asking a question: "Suffering from Knee Pain?" Another is by promising a benefit: "Get Back Pain Relief Now!" A third way is by delivering news: "Pain Relief Solution Found!" Finally, you can use a how-to: "How to Get Pain Relief!" Right after you grab readers' attention with a headline, the sub headline needs to keep their attention, so that they will keep reading your message. Here you can play on emotional triggers, such as fear, trust, value, or gratification, in your wording; the more triggers you can touch, the more your message will resonate.

"How I lost 30 pounds in 30 days by eating great food and never feeling hungry at all."

"I learned French by spending less than 15 minutes a day on it, while driving to work, and
now I can speak like a local!"

"By following these simple steps, I was able to increase my profits by 225%, without having to spend more on advertising."

The Irresistible Offer

In the Irresistible Offer, you will present an actual sales pitch, but your audience doesn't want to hear about how wonderful you think your product or service is. Here, you want people to imagine themselves using and loving your product or service. It's about romancing the audience and sparking their vivid imagination, and this is where you present what you are actually selling.

You want to start with where they are (relate to the pain, problem, objection), before you move forward with your message. Here you can use your message to ask people questions they can agree on; you can establish that what you are offering will be a good fit for them. The more yes answers you can elicit from people, the closer you will be driving them to believe that your product becomes the "Hell, yes!" solution to their problems or needs!

Always use explanations, language, and terms that your target customer will understand and can relate to. It's important that you do not forget that. Not everyone has the knowledge about your product or service that you have, so it is necessary that you simplify your wording and explanations to make your prospect understand exactly what you are trying to say and are selling.

TIP: *To brush up on your copy-writing skills, start reading books on copy writing, such as* The Garry Halbert Letters, *Dan Kennedy's* Ultimate Sales Letter, *or* Breakthrough Advertising *by Gene Schwartz. They are all excellent guides that will give you all of the tools and knowledge you need to write better copy.*

Crush Objections

No matter what your offer is, people will have objections to buying it! They may feel challenged by the need, the price, the features, or the timing, or they simply may lack urgency, money, or trust.

In order to sell, you must know what your prospects' objections are going to be in advance and use your sales message to address these issues and crush them, one by one. What sales objections really mean is that your prospects quite simply don't have enough information to make an informed decision, in order to purchase your product or service. Your job is to get them that information in the clearest way possible.

By making a list of all of the concerns and objections that could stop someone from doing business with you, you will be ready to face them and crush them. Consider all of the angles your prospects may be looking at, and then answer these questions with your sales messages as clearly as possible by explaining exactly how your product or service will benefit them.

With the right perspective, you will be able to absolutely crush any objection that your prospects may have.

Bullet Points

Use bullet points to introduce the benefits and the benefits of the benefits of your offer. Remember, people want to know how what you are selling will benefit them and make them feel. Rarely are they interested in the specifics of your offer, unless it is to compare it to another offer.

It's better to use three or four bullet points for benefits, rather than have a huge laundry list, to keep your prospect's interest. If you need more, break them into groups of three or four and distribute them throughout your sales message.

Bullet point benefits help engage your audience, and benefits address the outcome people will get from your offer.

Guarantee and Trial Period

The less risk a prospect sees in doing business with you, the sooner he or she will buy, because you're adding peace of mind to the shopper's experience.

To promote more trust in your product or service, you should always offer some kind of a guarantee; for example, you may offer a "30-Day Money Back," "No Questions Asked," "100% Satisfaction Guarantee" to a "Low Price Guarantee" or a free trial period to take the risk out of the purchase.

A strong money-back guarantee is an incredibly powerful sales and marketing tool. Offer a strong guarantee, and display it in all of your advertising. If your competition offers a guarantee, do everything you can to make your guarantee stronger.

Most important of all, if you offer a guarantee, following through on it! As with your sales message, do not promise something you can't or won't follow through on. It will erode your hard-earned trust, and word will spread quickly that you do not honor your promise.

Interestingly, refund rates are lower among customers who have purchased physical products, rather than virtual products. So if you are selling a product that could be delivered digitally, it's a good idea to actually include a physical product such as a CD, a DVD, a book, or a workbook that you ship to your client, to cut down on the refund rate.

Reviews and Testimonials

To drive the trust and risk point forward, take into consideration additional mediums and factors. It's important to highlight testimonials and reviews from previous customers showing how they have benefited from the use of your product; these are a great method of gaining customer trust.

Videos or images of before-and-after situations or of customers telling the viewer directly about their experience are some of the most dramatic ways to show the benefits of your product and reassure your customer about the validity of your claims. Using testimonials from industry experts or leaders can add an extra layer of credibility and assurance to your testimonials and reviews.

Always Use a Call to Action

Always make sure you cap off all of your messages or ads with a call to action or CTA. The call to action should be simple, yet effective. It should have a minimum of carefully chosen words; the less cluttered, the better. It should clearly and rapidly communicate exactly what you want the reader to do.

Calls to action may include "Sign up for more info," "Download now," "Buy it now," or "Add to cart."

The call to action should stand out from the rest of your design and attract attention from the moment a viewer first lands on a Web page. That way, the reader always knows it's there; the moment he or she is pushed over the edge into deciding to purchase, the action is only a click away.

But remember, you can also use it in subtle ways, as Vitamix did with its "Shop Products" link. Use your calls to action in a way that they will be most effective for your target market.

Your calls to action should tell readers exactly what's in it for them. Use confident language. Be bold and assertive, but stay congruent to your brand's style and tone.

The more engaging your message is, the more likely your customers will be to follow your call to action. You always need to lead your prospects in the direction you want them to go. That's why it's so important to guide them to it by using a CTA.

Calls to actions are surprisingly effective, yet are very often forgotten by the marketer.

Video

One way to significantly increase your sales, engagement, search engine rankings, and trust in your company is through video. Most people today would rather watch a video than read text, and they also perceive the value of video at a higher level.
Studies have shown that people buy sooner when they watch a product video.

You gain an edge over your competitors by investing in videos that explain and promote your products and services by using the same formulas we have used for writing effective copy, selling benefits over features, using calls to action, and offering testimonials from customers.

The great thing is that you don't need to invest in expensive video cameras or lighting equipment. You probably already own a smartphone with an HD camera built in. If you invest $20 in an external microphone and use natural light, you will have all you need to film great video anywhere.

TIP: *When shooting video in natural light, do not use harsh direct sunlight. Opt for "open shade," that sweet spot between sun and shade, just inside the shade ... facing the light, so that your subject will be illuminated by light, but not actually in the light.*

Split-Test Everything

Once you start marketing, don't simply send off a sales message into the void without checking the results. Be sure to use tracking pixels set on all of your Web pages, ads, and email offers, so that you know exactly which ads and sales messages are getting results.

Split-testing is where you take a message, image, or call to action and you test to see how it does in comparison with another you've exchanged it for, in order to come up with the perfect formula, so that people browsing your offer become buyers of your products—in short, "conversion."

Split-testing can be done for virtually any element of your Web page, from the headlines to the images you use, all the way to the call-to-action button. Adding or removing a word in a headline can have a huge impact; even the colors used on the checkout buttons are important.

A split test on a call-to-action button that used exactly the same wording, "Get started now," tested a red and a green button. The red button did 38 percent better on conversion. Even the placement of the button can make a different. In a test, the check-out button placed above a certain video did better than when it was placed below. Everything from the trial period to the free offer to the design of your page layout can be tested and checked to see which version converts to sales the best.

When done right, split-testing can increase your conversion rate by thousands of percentage points. It is of major importance, because many times the results totally defy any logic or personal preference.

Do your split-testing systematically; always use a "control offer" (an offer or a page that is already converting to sales well), and keep track of all of the changes and the percentages gained with each change. Eventually, you may be able to increase your conversions by 1,000 percent. The more you split-test and track the results, the higher your conversion numbers will get.

Split-testing is an absolute must when you're running ads of any kind online. If you are doing offline ads, send people to a specific offer page that has been created for that particular offer or a phone number that is unique to each ad you are publishing, so that you can track all of the results. (There are online phone services that will rent you a phone number and will track the incoming calls.)

If you're not measuring the effectiveness of your ads or the offers you make, you are literally throwing away the most important data you could be collecting. If you don't measure what is or isn't working, you are just guessing.

Go to Where Your Customer Is

You never know where the consumer will be at any point in time, so you have to find a way to be everywhere. If you are having success on other sales platforms that you've been test-selling on . . . keep selling on them!

Even though you have set up your own website, it's a good idea keep selling on the proven platforms, such as Amazon, eBay, and Etsy. Although sales may shrink a bit once your website marketing efforts pick up, these platforms will still drive customers to your site, so it's important not to give up on them.

The more places where prospects can find your product or service, the better off you are.

Right now, one of the best ways to have people engage with your product online is to build a following by using social media to eventually drive people to your website or to offers, in order to build your email list. You will have to embrace a few social media platforms, focus your efforts on getting your message out there, and start creating a community and a presence.

The following sections will give you a quick overview of what the various social media platforms do, so that you can find the ones that match your niche or demographic the best.

Facebook

The largest and most important of all social media platforms right now is, of course, Facebook. With over 2 billion members, no other social media platform comes close to its reach and importance. One in every five page views in the United States is on Facebook. If you have any kind of product or service, you should have a Facebook fan page or group where you can engage your customers.

One of the great things about having a Facebook fan page is that you get access to your own Audience Insights demographics data regarding who is engaging with your fan page, where they are coming from, what they are buying, and which posts get the best engagement (likes, comments, and shares). As a result, you will be able to use that data to target your posts better.

All of the posts you write should have your target audience in mind; your posts should be short and attention grabbing. Quotes and image quotes are a great way to get the message out; people love to share quotes! Make sure to always put your logo and website URL on your images and quotes. Finally, always ask yourself: Is the post interesting? What would my target audience think?

TIP: A great Facebook posting strategy is to check the FB Audience Insight data and then "reissue" the posts that have gained the best fan engagement, by posting them over and over again (at intervals of about three to four weeks). This will help you build an audience. Boosting your post so that it becomes a "suggested post" is another way to create a broader audience for your page, because Facebook's organic reach is not as great, due to Facebook's focusing more on the pay-for-views model.

LinkedIn

For professionals and businesses, LinkedIn is a place to connect and network. Every Fortune 500 company has a presence, and so should you. LinkedIn is more specifically geared toward professionals and is used mainly for business networking. One of the main features of the site is to allow users to keep a list of connections with people whom they have had a past business relationship. LinkedIn is also unique, in that it is a job marketplace and is often used as leverage in job interviews.

No matter what business you are in, you will want to fill out your LinkedIn Profile. As mentioned earlier, LinkedIn is a networking site for professionals. Think of it as a Facebook for professionals, but recent college graduates are the fastest-growing demographic.

It's a great place to network B to B or professional to professional. Add a professional-looking photo and keep it updated with your and your company's latest offerings and achievements. It's also a great place to post business-related articles and content, including videos . . . all of which can lead people back to your site. LinkedIn is a great place to advertise B to B as well.

Remember, you are using all of these social media platforms to build awareness of who you are and what you do, by adding content that people want.

Google+

Although Google+, with its 500 million members, has nowhere near the same reach as Facebook, do not ignore the power behind the Google brand name and its integration with other Google-owned products, such as search and YouTube. The social platform is the same, in the sense that you can find your friends and family, share pictures, post videos, and make comments. In addition, just as with Twitter, you can follow people, including those you don't know, such as celebrities. Unlike Twitter, however, there are no word limits to your posts.

Twitter

Twitter has quickly become the platform of choice for news, product launches, and venting customer service problems. It is a social media platform you should be monitoring to be sure you deliver what your customer expects from you! As a micro blogging service, this platform is particularly useful for individuals who lead very busy lives but still want to update their friends, family, or fan base.

Twitter users post more than 750 tweets a second. People tweet about the news, they tweet about their travels, they tweet about what they are doing right now, they rave about products. They will also rant and complain about bad service, a problem with a product, or bad customer service, and it can spread like wildfire!!

Although the tweets are only 140 characters long, they can have a huge impact, both positive and negative, so it's important to be on top of things, monitoring what is said about your product or service. A great way to get a following on Twitter is for your company or product to have its own #hashtag (make it a memorable one and make it visible!). Once again, use high-quality images, keep your tweets to the point, and make sure they resonate with your product's image and consumer. Keep an eye on what people are saying about your product or service, and always use #hashtags, especially your own!

TIP: *Twitter is a great place to practice your headline-writing skills, given that you have only 140 characters to get your message across. The better you learn to engage your followers on Twitter with your tweets, the better your headline-writing skills will get!*

YouTube

YouTube is one of the Internet powerhouses, second in searches only to its owner, Google, with thousands of videos uploaded every second. It's where people go not only to look for entertainment and engaging content, but also to find answers to problems. YouTube is a huge opportunity! So be sure you take advantage of it.

It is somewhat of a social media platform in disguise. Google loves YouTube and displays its videos in its search results, with thumbnails of your videos that make you stand out from the crowd in the search results.

Using video in your marketing nowadays is key to your online success! Most people prefer to watch a quick, engaging video over reading a long article.

Having a YouTube channel can increase traffic to your website exponentially, so no matter what product or service you are offering, you should set up a YouTube channel. On it, you can post valuable content, teach something, help solve problems, or simply have fun and engage your audience.

If you want to see a perfect example of a creative and fun use of a YouTube channel, head over to the Blendtec YouTube channel. Blendtec's blender sales took off, and the product started to sell millions because of the "Will It Blend?" videos on YouTube that went viral. I highly recommend that you take a minute and look at some of them. They are as creative and original as one can get when marketing a product that is normally totally boring.

Think of what content you could share on YouTube. How could you add value for your prospects and make your product fun and engaging?
Videos on tips about how to do something or how to solve a problem add huge value, are very easy to produce, and don't have to be very long at all. Use videos to explain the benefits of your products or services. Remember to add as much value for the visitor as you can. And be sure to always put a call to action and to add your URL at the end of the video so that people can get more information.

Always make sure that your video has great audio. As crazy as it seems, good clear audio is actually more important than good video quality, so always use a high-quality microphone when recording your videos.

Be sure to tag and check that your video description below the actual video is filled out and is keyword rich, because Google loves adding YouTube to its search results. Optimize the keywords for searches on each video you put on your YouTube channel, to make it easy for Google to index them. Best of all, Google will index your page by placing a small thumbnail image of your video next to the search result, so that your video post will stand out among the other search results.

It's also a good idea to get a transcript made of the audio portion of your video. This can be easily done online for a few dollars and can add immense value for your clients and you, because you can repurpose it for blogs, books, reports, and so on. And if you post it in the description below the video, Google will use the description as keywords!

TIP: *Think of the ten most frequently asked questions you get about your product or service, and answer those on a video. Then think about ten questions people should be asking themselves about your product or services, and make ten more videos answering those questions.*

Pinterest

Pinterest is where mainly women go for inspiration and ideas when it comes to fashion, food, travel, and home decorations. If you are in one of these niches, you should be pinning your designs, your products, and even recipes to drive traffic back to your website. Think of pinning a photo to a tack board. That is how this site operates. Of the top ten websites similar to Facebook, this is by far the most visual. In fact, it is mostly composed of photos that are shared across boards, with small captions underneath.

If you are in the fashion, accessories, home decor, travel, or food niche, Pinterest will be one of the sites that can help drive traffic back to your site. Note that 68 percent of its users are women, and 50 percent are mothers who "pin" and collect images of things they like and dream of on their Pinterest boards. Here, your main objective is to have very high-quality, magazine-like images and designs and witty quotes that feed your consumers' dreams. You always want the name of your company or URL on the image itself, and include hyperlinks. Make sure that your boards have fun and original titles that are related to your items to make them stand out as likable and sharable!

TIP: *If you are a photographer, an artist, or an illustrator, besides pinning your images on Pinterest, you can expose your images and designs on Flicker, Tumbler or Instagram.*

Instagram

Instagram is quickly becoming a powerhouse for images and videos that can bring awareness to your products or services. It is very much liked by the fashion and foodie crowd. Much like Pinterest, Instagram is a platform to share photos. What differs, however, is that these are mostly candid and not stock footage. It allows users to upload and edit pictures, as well as share them to other platforms on this list. The main feature of this social network is the extensive ability to edit and play with your pictures, so always be sure to use great, high-quality images.

Yelp

Yelp is perhaps one of the only social networking sites that incorporates a sense of real life. Users log on to write reviews about any place they have eaten, traveled, slept, and so on. These reviews show up in the main feed on the user's profile, where other people can privately comment or reward you with a compliment. There are also statistics on the ratings for your reviews. This is entirely unique to Yelp. As with most other social media sites, people can also upload pictures, which they usually post with their reviews.

Yelp is considered one of the top ten websites, similar to Facebook, because it encourages users to display their real names, pictures, and information. This simultaneously adds validity to any reviews posted.

Podcasting

Day by day, more experts are preaching the gospel of podcasting as a content marketing tool. It's a very enticing idea to have your own prerecorded radio show that your audience can listen to when they're working out or driving in the car.

Every minute that a customer or a prospect listens to us speak with authority, we're establishing ourselves as a thought-leader. Conceptually, the more time our audience spends with our content, the more authority we have as content marketers.

Podcasting may seem complicated and like a lot of work, but it doesn't have to be. You don't need a super-expensive microphone, nor do you need a fancy-sound mixing board. All you need is a willingness to be open and honest and deliver consistent value to the consumers your business serves.

TIP: *If getting your message out there via a podcast is not enough enticement, remember that you can get your podcasts transcribed and reuse the content on other platforms, repurposing them as blog posts, social media posts, and tweets. Transcriptions can even be repurposed as reports and even books.*

Social Media Best Practices

Now that you know what the main social media platforms are, pick two or three of these platforms that best match your dream customer demographic and embrace them, because you will need to give them all of the attention you can. You will constantly have to post and engage your audience to keep them interested in what you are offering.

Your social media postings should add value and keep your audience engaged. Openness goes a long way in social media. It's a big part of building trust with your community. An engaged audience is one of the greatest assets a company can have. This is why you need to focus on only a few platforms!

Social media platforms offer the potential to increase your public profile because they're all about relationships. Keep the social in social media. This seems like it would be obvious, yet many people using social media don't get social with their followers. Should you engage with your brand's influencers? Yes! Should you engage with your customers? Always! Should you engage with everyone who reaches out to you? Indeed!

The main reason you are using social media is to drive viewers from there to your site. If you are offering them good information, you're building rapport and trust so that they get to know you, your brand, and your products better.

It's important to keep posting all the time, to keep your followers engaged.
Big companies have professional departments dedicated to this, but you can either do it yourself or outsource part of it by using a virtual assistant who can post and reply to comments and monitor your followers.

Luckily, a few tools out there will let you automate your social media postings, much in the same way that your email auto responder does with your email campaigns. These let you schedule posts and upload media to various sites with one click. HootSuite.com lets you schedule posts to all social media sites from one single place. To upload videos to all sites, Oneload.com or Trafficgeyser.com lets you upload to all of the video sites from one location.

The more you can automate your social media, the better. Yet remember, even though you automate it, you will still need to monitor your comments and negative feedback!

Negative and Positive Feedback

Though it may be tempting to respond to positive feedback and delete the negative, don't. Instead, respond to all feedback in a positive manner, thank your community for sharing your content or recommending your products, and invite members to share their stories through interviews or as guest bloggers on your site.

If you receive negative feedback, consider it to be constructive criticism and an opportunity to improve. If someone is complaining, it's more than likely the person is looking for a resolution from you. Very rarely do people merely want to complain. Therefore, respond as quickly as possible and avoid the urge to purge.

Design and Message Congruency

When you are going to be everywhere, you need to focus on keeping the design identity and the message of your business congruent with that of your website and product on all social media platforms that you post to. Use the same logos, images, and voice in your messages, on the social media sites you have chosen.

To simplify this process, there are design services such as Tweetpages that keep all of your social media branding in sync.

Always have links back to your website, and be sure to use watermarks of your logo or URL on all of the images and quotes you use on social media, so that people will always know where the image came from and will know where to go to find out more.

Advertising

Lots of people hope that putting up a website and setting up a Facebook fan page will automatically start to drive sales on their website. Nothing is further from the truth. While social media may help a bit to get your name out there and get people to engage with you, the key to driving traffic to your site and generating sales is advertising!

The great thing is that most social media platforms can be used to send extremely targeted advertising messages.

Facebook Advertising

In the last few years, Facebook ads have become the platform of choice for online marketers, and for good reason. Never before has a small business owner had so much powerful advertising demographic data at his or her fingertips.

You now are able to target your ads to reach a target market by selecting people's particular interests, age, gender, geographic location, education level, language, relationship status, movie likes, page likes, previous purchases, and spending habits.

You can pinpoint and target the exact audience demographic you're trying to reach with your product or service. Never before has this level of laser-targeting been available to a small business owner. This makes it possible to focus on or target the people most likely to be interested in the product, among the 2 billion people worldwide on Facebook.

Facebook advertising is a game changer for small businesses.

Chapter 6

When you set up your Facebook ads, your main focus will be finding the target market you are going after. By using Facebook's Audience Insights tool in the FB Ads Manager, you will be able to pinpoint exactly who your target market is (remember the surfer example from Chapter 2). By now, you should already be familiar with the Audience Insights tool, because you should have done some of your demographical research using it. By inputting the names of other brands and products, thought leaders, events, organizations, and associations into the "Interests" field, you will be able to see exactly who the target audience of your competition is. If you add more interests, your ad audience gets even more targeted. (If you go to back to Chapter 2, you'll find an example of how to use "Interests" to target your market.)

NOTE: *If you have a Facebook fan page, the Page Insights will give you the exact target audience that is engaging with your page.*

Advertising on Facebook does not have to cost much, depending on how you set it up. Either you are doing CPC (cost per click, where you pay only when someone clicks on your ad) or CPM (where you pay per thousand ads served). Which one you use depends on what you are promoting, but usually you will do a CPC and let FB optimize the amount to spend per click. Start off with a $20 budget and see what the response is to your ad; then scale it up, depending on the ROI (return on investment) you are getting.

When advertising anywhere online, always use tracking pixels so that you can gauge what impact your ads are having. "You can't manage what you don't measure." On Facebook, this is truer than ever before, because FB gives you so much more laser-targeted demographic information and tracking that you can use to optimize your advertising efforts.

Remember that in order to engage people browsing Facebook, the image you use in your ads needs to be attention grabbing. Think high-contrast images and square. Images with colorful backgrounds, black-and-white images (yes . . . B&W attracts attention in a colored world!). Images of people looking straight into the camera and smiling, as well as animals, work best at grabbing attention and stand out from the crowded Facebook news feed.

As always, your headline has to be engaging, short, and full of impact! Because you have only twenty-five characters for your ad headline, you really need to hone your message. While you can write as much as you want on a Facebook-promoted post, you will want to have your call to action and your URL show before the ". . . read more" link, so make sure you have both in the first two lines of your message. (It's good to use a URL shortener, so that you can track clicks to your ads in more than one way.) This is because you want people to be able to click on the link to your offer without having to click on the ". . . read more" link, no matter what device they are browsing on. It's especially important to use high-impact images that will grab the Facebook browser's attention.

Capitalizing your words and using descriptive domain name URL's and extensions will reinforce your headline even more.

NOTE: *It is of utmost importance that the images you use in Facebook ads and posts have a very high-impact value, no matter whether you are using them in a newsfeed ad or a right-hand-side ad. But remember, if you are using text in them, don't use more than 20 percent of your image as text, because FB will not approve it, if you plan on using it for an ad. FB has a 20 percent limit on how much text you can display in an ad image.*

Measure the impact that your ad is having. If people are clicking on your ad, then you are doing something right. If people are not clicking, first try changing the image you are using and see how it goes, then change the headline. Test and tweak your ad till you get the results you are looking for.

After you have had an ad running for a certain amount of time, you may have a drop in clicks. Ads have a set life cycle: some may work for a week, others for a month. When you see a drop in the click-through rate (CTR), it's time to change the image. You do not need to change the copy or the headline if it has worked for you before.

The great thing about online advertising is that if you use CPC (cost per click), you pay only when someone clicks on your ad, making it a very cost-effective way of advertising. The other option is CPM (cost per thousand impressions), where you are paying less, but you pay for each time someone sees your ad. To sell products online, it's recommended that you use CPC.

TIP: After you have done one full day of advertising on FB, it's time to run an FB Ads Report, so that you can see exactly who is clicking on and engaging with your ads. By analyzing the age, gender, shares, comments, and checkouts, you now can narrow the targeting of your ads even further. By adjusting the targeting of the age group and the gender of the people who are clicking, sharing, commenting, and buying your offer, you will be able to increase your conversion rate by many percentage points.

Google Paid Search

Google AdWords works in that you bid on keywords (a word used by a search engine in its search for relevant Web pages), in order to serve your ad. When a person searches for that word, your ad is served, and when your ad is clicked on, you get charged, and it leads the searcher to your website.

Advertisers compete against one another in the Google AdWords auction for select keywords; the bid prices for using certain keywords in your ads depend greatly on the relevance of the keyword at any given time. Advertisements will appear primarily above or to the right-hand side of organic listings, and the position where your ad appears depends on the amount you have bid and the budget you have selected for using it.

Getting your site to rank near the top of the listings on Google is part science, part art.
Both Facebook and Google Ads are quickly and easily updatable and changed, and it's very easy to see whether they are having an effect. They both have very good metrics pages, where you can monitor everything and see whether people are interested in your offer. You will want to make sure your ROI (return on investment) on the cost per click is viable.

Setting Up Your Google Ad

http://adwords.google.com/keywordplanner

The keyword planner tool lets you see which word or phrase people search for most often on Google. What you want to do is type in the keyword for your product or service, and see which search terms are most popular in your category to discover what people are actually searching for.

Select keywords with the highest search volume—that is, the word that is highest in the minds of people looking for your product or service.

When you create your campaign, it is important to—in broad terms—lay the foundation. As your campaign accumulates data, you can zero in on the keywords driving the strongest ROI. If necessary, expand on these top-performing keywords with like terms. Meanwhile, pause keywords that are driving poor traffic or driving a weak ROI.

You can find the audience that's most interested in your product or service by understanding the three major groups of online searchers: *Browsers* are people searching for general information. It's usually hard to tell what exactly each person is looking for. One person might be doing research for a term paper. Another person might be killing time, waiting for a bus. The vast majority in this group aren't ready to buy and probably never will be.
Shoppers are definitely interested in your product, but they're still at the research stage, checking out reviews and comparing prices. Some folks from this group will be ready to buy in a matter of days or even hours, but for others, it may be weeks, months, or possibly never.

Buyers are typing with one hand and holding their credit card in the other. They know exactly what they want, and the only barrier to making a purchase is finding the right place and the right deal.
So, how do you tell which of these three groups a person is in? By studying the keywords they enter into the search bar. As a general rule of thumb, the more specific the search, the closer they are to the "buyer" group.

Take, for instance, the three different types of people searching for a phone:

A browser will search for keywords containing just one or two words with no modifiers:

- Phone
- Smartphones

A shopper is a bit more specific, using modifiers that will help find sites containing a greater depth of information:

- iPhone Smartphone reviews
- Best iPhone Smartphone
- iPhone X Plus Smartphone
- iPhone Smartphone compare

Finally, the buyer is very specific, often using the results of his previous research in the keywords:

- Order iPhone X
- Buy online iPhone X
- Apple iPhone X best price

If you're just getting started with your AdWords campaigns and budget is your biggest concern, it makes sense to target only the buyer group. These folks are the easiest to convert to customers. As your experience grows, you can extend your reach to the shoppers and, to some degree, even to the browsers as well.

Some third-party tools will allow you to dig even deeper, by figuring out what your competitors are bidding on and feeding the data back to you. There are plenty of software applications to choose from. SEMrush, SpyFu, AdGooroo, WordStream, and Wordtracker are each helpful in their own way.

While your ad position strategy may differ from the norm, it is a best practice to have your ad show within the first three ad placements available. To ensure that your average position stays within this range, adjusting keyword bids should be a weekly task. For keywords falling below this range, increase their bids by 10 to 15 percent, using your best judgment. Keywords that fall well below this range—think position 5.0 and lower—may not be worth increasing to achieve a position within the top three if they will jeopardize your average CPC; however, it may not hurt to keep them running, either.

For keywords that maintain a 1.0 average position, try decreasing bids by 5 percent. This will ensure that these keywords stay within the specified range but are not unnecessarily increasing your average CPC to maintain a position of 1.0.

Negative Keywords

Depending on how much traffic you receive through PPC, negative keywords should be added on a weekly basis. This is part and parcel of ensuring that you are receive quality traffic, get in front of the right audience, and also that your ads are not being shown for keywords they should not be shown for. Google AdWords Help explains how to choose and use negative keywords

Potential negative keywords can be identified by sifting through search term reports at the overall account level, the individual campaign level, and the ad group level. If your campaign is well-organized from a keyword/ad group perspective, adding negative keywords at the campaign level is the most efficient practice.

Much like identifying negative keywords by examining search term reports, you can also mine for converting search terms. You can capture leads through search terms that you have not yet added as exact or phrase match types to your campaign. The next step is to add these terms as exact or phrase match keywords and to regularly do so on a weekly or biweekly basis, similar to adding negative keywords. The benefit of adding converting search terms is typically an improved conversion rate. Combined with the addition of negative keywords, you should see an increase in quality traffic and less wasted *spend* (expense).

How much you are willing to invest in your campaign is a key influencer of what you can expect to receive: conversions. Without careful distribution and redistribution, you could quickly see your ROI decrease.

The most important factor in any advertising is the ROI (return on investment). What's the point in an advertising campaign if it doesn't boost your return on investment? After all, if you put in $1,000 toward a marketing campaign, but in the end you get only an extra $500 in revenue and no guarantees of return or loyal customers, that's $500 wasted (and much more, if you account for the time and effort you invested).
Do your homework, though, and make sure that even the worst case scenario will be in your favor financially; calculate the link between marketing spend vs. customer acquisition, engagement, retention, and value.

Retargeting

You never want to let the people who visited your site simply leave and forget about you. This is where retargeting and lead capture come in. With retargeting, when someone visits your site, a piece of code is placed onto his or her Web browser, and your ads will follow that person around the Internet to different websites that are Google affiliates: blogs, news pages, forums, and even over to Facebook, which hopefully will eventually drive them back to your offer or website. See Fig. 6.1.

Retargeting is extremely effective and extremely cheap, because once again you pay for the ad only if someone clicks on it. Best of all, this makes it look as if you're spending a ton of money on advertising!

You can retarget with Google directly in the AdsManager and in Facebook, where you would use a third-party solution, such as PerfectAudience or Adroll.

Chapter 6

Email Marketing

Contrary to what you may think, email marketing is very, very effective! But your email list is only as good as the number of people who actually open your emails and engage with you!

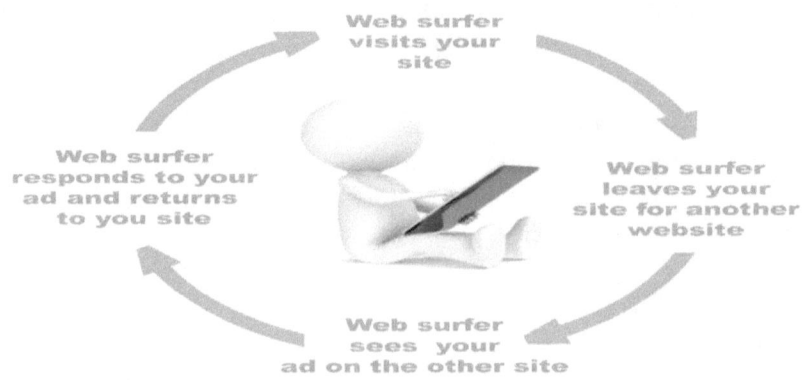

Fig. 6.1.

Your social media and advertising efforts should be driving traffic back to your website or, better yet, a squeeze page, where you will ethically bribe the visitor to opt into your mailing list with content such as ebooks, reports, and video guides that provides them with valuable or entertaining information. If the information is enticing enough (and is perceived as valuable), the prospects will have no problem exchanging their information for your offer.

Once people have shown interest in what you offer by opting into your mailing list in exchange for whatever offer you "bribed" them with, you will need to get your message through the marketing clutter to keep the conversation going. This is where the strength of your copywriting and attention-grabbing skills will be tested! Now you will have to stand out from the crowd in people's inboxes, so that you do not end up in the trash!

The Subject Line

Your main attention-getting "headline" in your emails is going to be your subject line. Your main mission is to grab the attention of your target customer right away, so that this person is intrigued into opening your email. It's no easy task! Just as with regular junk mail, people usually go through their email by immediately throwing away or deleting mail that looks like junk; they keep and open only those that look important or personal.

So, how do you grab people's attention and stand out from the crowd so that they will open your email?
The trick is to do unusual things with your subject lines that make them stand out in a full email inbox. The key is to make the email look more personal, so that it will appear different from the others, visually. Usually, simplicity and brevity win.

Sometimes you can use simple tricks, such as subject lines that have only the person's name and/or an emoji smiley face, to make your email look like a personal message.

For example:
Subject: John ;o)

Other times, it can be a short attention grabber, where you just use one or tow words in caps: IMPORTANT! or DUMB MISTAKE or UNBELIEVABLE. A subject that looks as if it is important will make the prospect want to read more to find out what is so earth-shattering.

For example:
Subject: DUMB MISTAKE!

The Message

Here, once again, this is where your copy-writing talent will need to prove itself.

But once you have gotten people to open the email, you have to nail it with your message or offer, in order to engage them. You can provide great information that is relevant to the reason they opted in or make irresistible offers they can't refuse.

The goal of your email is to build customer and client satisfaction and reinforce the belief that signing up or buying was a good idea. Delight people with something awesome they weren't expecting in all of your emails, and, if you can, make it as relevant as possible to the idea or the reason they opted in for. Ideally, this would be an add-on, a next-steps resource, or an exercise to help them even further—it could come in a worksheet, checklist, video, audio, report, guide, or even tip sheet format.

The idea is to make people even happier they took action—even if they have done nothing yet or haven't even looked at the item they bought or opted in for.

You should have a sequence of emails set up on your email auto responder, mapping out a process, so that once somebody opts in, he or she is taken though your "Sales Funnel."

TIP: *Sign up for the email lists of the top Internet marketers, such as Frank Kern, Eban Pagan, or Jeff Walker, and study the copy they are writing, then model what they are doing! One of the reasons they make so much money is that they are masters of email marketing messages and strategies!*

Reengaging Old Prospects or Customers

One of the best email reengaging strategies I have heard of was created by Dean Jackson. It's called the nine-word email. This is all that it implies: nine words that engage the person, opening a conversation by getting him or her to answer a simple question.

It can be used to reengage people who have abandoned shopping carts or those you haven't heard from in a while. You're able to drive a "dead list" into a "new list" at the same time.

Something as simple as the person's name in the subject line and then a simple phrase, such as "Hey, there, are you still looking to lose weight?" or "Peter, are you still looking for a new car?" can generate response rates of more than 80 percent. It is that simple, because the message looks personal and nonthreatening. The great thing is, this takes less than a few minutes to set up, does not even have to be nine words . . . and gets amazing results!

Just so there is no confusion, it would look like Fig. 6.2, nothing more, nothing less!

The key to using this strategy is not to deviate from its simplicity, because that is what makes it effective. It looks like a short, quick personal message . . . and not like a carefully crafted or thought-out one.

Chapter 6

Email List Building

One of the biggest questions is, how does one get a list of prospects' email addresses in the first place? In the online world, this is called "list building," and it is the Holy Grail of all online marketers!

Basically, everything you have been doing so far—finding your target market, finding your product, building your dream customer avatar, designing your website, setting up an email auto responder service, setting up your social media presence, writing your blog, posting on social media, learning how to write great headlines and copy, and advertising on Google and Facebook—has been built and set up so that you can get people to opt into your email list, from which you will do the bulk of your selling and marketing.

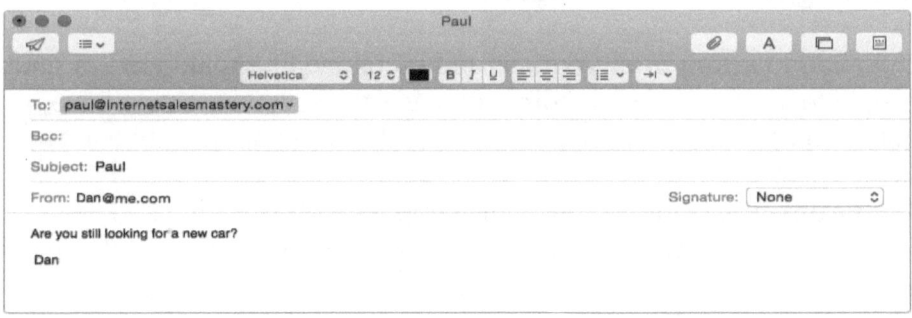

Fig. 6.2
(View full-size color image at www.internetsalesmastery.com/book_images.html)

The way you will convince people to give you their email address is by offering them something of high value, in what online marketers call the "ethical bribe." This could be a free PDF report, a book, a sample product, an assessment, a free trial period, a series of videos, or anything else that your target audience will desire and see as a useful, high-quality offer.

Remember, this is probably going to be the first time you make contact with your future clients, so whatever you are giving has to be of the highest quality, to make a good first impression and so they will be happy to have given you their email address. It should be very helpful to them and should let them get to know you or your product better. It should be the start of a relationship that builds trust and rapport.

Think about your target market's greatest fears and desires. What keeps them up at night? Who do they want to become? What do they want? Then offer the solution in your free giveaway, be it in the form of a report, an ebook, a video series, or a trial period.

Landing and Squeeze Pages

Your call to action from your ads and social media should always send people to a lead capture, landing, or squeeze page, where they have only two options: to fill in their email address and name or to leave.

The beauty of a landing page is the simplicity of its design and setup. It basically can have the exact same message or promise on it that the ad or the post had, with the same call to action. Squeeze pages generate much higher opt-in rates than regular Web pages with opt-in fields, but in the end your opt-in rate is going to be determined by the quality of what you offer in exchange for the email address and how much it aligns with the hopes, needs, and desires of your target market.

Every business will need different data from its target audience, in order to market to them effectively, but remember that less is always better. The less information you ask for, the higher the chance of the visitor submitting the form.

Asking for the person's name and email address is the bare minimum, and if you can utilize just that data effectively, then go for it. When you start asking for more personal information, such as addresses and phone numbers, it will drastically reduce your opt-in rate.

Performance Tracking

One of the most beneficial features of any online marketing platform is the ability to track the performance of each email message that is sent out. You can view the open rate and the click-through rate of each message or ad that you create. This allows you to see how people on your list are reacting to each mailing or ad that you mail to them.

If the open rate is low, then there is possibly an issue with the subject line of the message. If the click-through rate is low, then the body of the email message was not effective.

This data allows you to continually improve the performance and effectiveness of your email marketing effort. Analyze each mailing, and try to learn something about your lists to use in your next mailing.

Campaigns vs. One-Off Ads and Emails

Always think campaigns, not one-off emails!

Whenever you advertise anywhere, online or offline, it's important to think in terms of campaigns: a coordinated series of linked advertisements or emails with a single idea or theme in mind. Be sure of your objectives before you dive into creating your ads.

The great thing about email campaigns is that you can automate them. All you need to do is load up your email auto responder with the marketing messages, and it will do the rest.

It's a good practice to set up your email auto responder to send out at least one or two emails a month with content that adds value to your prospect, be it videos, newsletters, or reports, so that you and your offer stay in the person's mind.

You will want to make sure you have at least six or twelve months' worth of great content ready to be emailed, so that when people opt into your list because of your "ethical bribe," you will automatically send them great content and irresistible offers that trickle into their email inbox every month for the next year without your having to think about it.

Not only does this give you more opportunities to engage with your customers, but it also lets you establish more rapport and trust. You do not have to stick to one single format; you can deliver video, audio, and info graphics, anything that will deliver value and will engage your prospect.

Statistics shows that 80 percent of sales occur after the fifth to twelfth contact! So be sure to set up an email campaign that will engage your prospects at least until the twelfth contact!

Offline Marketing

Even if you are selling online, you should also be marketing in the offline world!

While email inboxes keep getting more and more offers, regular mailboxes are getting fewer and fewer, so take advantage of that. Combine your online marketing with offline marketing channels, such as direct mail, newspaper advertising, specialty magazines, and so on.

When delivered via mail, a catalog or a marketing piece enhances the choosing or reading experience. Offline channels can drive highly qualified visitors back to the website with products in mind to purchase.

While it would take another book to teach you what you need to know to effectively market offline, the basics are pretty much the same. Focus on your target market, use clever headlines and images, use engaging copy, have a call to action (drive people back to your website!), and keep on marketing to them!

Executive Summary

TOP TEN TAKEAWAYS

1. For your marketing message to resonate, you will need to craft a very unique story that talks directly to your arget market.
2. Pick two or three social media platforms that match your niche or demographic the best and embrace them!
3. "You can't manage what you don't measure." When advertising anywhere online, always use tracking pixels so that you can gauge what impact your ads are having.
4. With Facebook, you are able to pinpoint and target the exact audience demographic for your ads.
5. Google Adwords works in that you bid on keywords (a word used by a search engine in its search for relevant Web pages) in order to serve your ad.
6. Your product, your brand, and your service should have a personality on social media.
7. Use retargeting to follow your website visitor around the Web with your ads.
8. Use a nine-word email to reengage with customers or leads.
9. Think in terms of campaigns, not one-off ads or emails.
10. Always make sure you cap off all of your marketing messages or ads with a call to action.

Chapter 6

SIMPLE ACTION STEPS TO TAKE

- Craft your marketing message as a story directed toward your dream customer avatar.
- Select two or three social media platforms, and start posting great, engaging content.
- Start advertising on Facebook, targeting your target markets, interests, age, and gender.
- Advertise on Google using keywords that are specific to your product or niche.
- Set up retargeting campaigns.
- Set up at least twelve months of emails that are specific to your target market.
- Use the nine-word email to reengage old customers and leads.

NOTES:

Chapter 7: Creating Sales Success

We covered a lot in the last chapter, because the better you can inform and prime your prospects with your marketing, the better the chance of a sale will be.

Yet the sad truth is that no matter how great your marketing is, no matter great your website is, no matter how irresistible or how unique your offer is, only about 2 percent of the people who visit your site or store will end up buying from you right away!

This means 98 out of 100 will simply leave your website and go and do something else.

But the good news it that about 15 percent of those who inquire about a product or a service will buy the product or the service in the next 90 days, 20 percent will take 12 months to make up their minds, and 50 percent of the people who inquire about a product or a service will buy it within 18 months.

This means that 85 percent of the people will buy a product or a service, if, and only if, you remarket to them. The real value and the bulk of your sales are in the 85 percent of those prospects!

In this chapter, we will go over how to find your unique selling proposition, how to build rapport, and how to gain the trust of your prospects. I will teach you some buying triggers and also show you how to overcome objections, in order to help you convert prospects into clients.

Presenting Your Offer

People buy products based on their desires (to stand out, to look glamorous, and so on), not on their needs.

You need to know what motivates your customers' behavior and buying decisions. Effective marketing requires you to be an amateur psychologist. You need to know what drives and motivates customers.

Go beyond the traditional customer demographics that most businesses collect to analyze their sales trends. For example, for an online T-shirt shop, it's not enough to know that 75 percent of your customers are in the eighteen-to-twenty-five age range. You need to look at their motives for buying T-shirts, such as fashion statements, convenience, price, and many others.

Very few businesses are one of a kind. Just look around you. How many clothing retailers, electronics stores, air conditioning installers, and electricians are truly unique?

The key to effective selling in this situation is what advertising and marketing professionals call a "unique selling proposition" (USP). Unless you can pinpoint what makes your business unique in the world of homogeneous competitors, you cannot target your sales efforts successfully.

Uncover Your Unique Selling Proposition (USP)

If you have ever heard of or used Zappos, the online shoe company, you probably know its USP: risk-free buying. Zappos offers to ship products to you for free and lets you return anything that did not fit or you simply did not like for free as well. Zappos asks no questions . . . and makes it hassle free. The company makes sure its customer service is the best and most fun out there. That is its USP.
Tom's Shoes have a USP that you rarely see. Toms Shoes are quirky, comfy, light, and inexpensive. That alone probably isn't enough to make a company stand out in the shoe business. The unique and compelling part of the Tom's Shoes proposition is that the company gives a new pair of shoes to a child in need for every pair you purchase. You don't even have to remember the exact words. The story is what sticks in your head.

The USP of Warby Parker, an eyeglass company, is to send you six frames for free that you can try on at home for a week, so you can see which will suit you best. Amazon's USP is a giant selection of anything you can think of, its low prices, and its super-fast shopping.

How can you differentiate yourself from the competition? How can you position your business to highlight your USP? Why would someone want to buy your product or service? What could your unique selling proposition be? What is something that sets you apart? What can you promote that will make customers want to patronize your business?

Selling

In a way, selling is basically a contact sport, but in another way, selling is more like any relationship. You need to build trust and rapport with your customer, and you need to keep on nurturing that relationship at all times.

Sales conversion statistics occur like this: about 2 percent of your website visitors will buy right away, 3 percent will take you up on your offer on the 2nd contact, 5 percent on the 3rd, 10 percent on the 4th contact, but the bulk, 80 percent of your prospects, will buy from you on the 5th to 12th contact. Hence the need of using an email auto responder system and setting it up with campaigns containing at least twelve engaging emails.

The amazing thing is that 92 percent of people and companies give up on their prospects on the 5th contact!

Knowing this will already give you that edge over most of your competition, because you now realize that you need to keep remarketing to your prospects over and over again, via email, social media, and Facebook and Google and retargeting ads.

Remarketing

Remarketing is one of the key online and offline techniques to boost sales conversion rates and is arguably the most profitable marketing technique there is. The great thing is that online with your website, you have ways to remarket and stay in contact with EVERYONE who came to your website.

You should be remarketing to everyone, from people who have just visited your website and left, to those who actually showed some interest and opted in to get your free offer, the newsletter or the report, to those who for some reason abandoned their shopping carts, and, most important, you should be remarketing to people who already bought from you.

And because you are using tracking pixels on all of your pages and in your emails and ads' email, you can remarket to all of them, even those who did not sign up for a free offer. I already have covered all you need to know about email marketing and email reengagement and how to use retargeting to stay on the Web browser's mind, both mentioned in the previous chapter, so now we are going to concentrate on the missing parts.

Keep Selling to Existing Customers

Mot people tend to forget about their existing customers after selling to them, and when they do, it is always to their detriment. Most of the time, their focus on gaining customers and/or market share is their main goal for every marketing campaign they undertake. But then they forget to market to the customers they already have, because most marketers are focused on the transactional value and not thinking of the lifetime value of a customer.

The customer lifetime value (CLV) is the amount of revenue or profit a customer generates over his or her entire lifetime. Knowing the CLV is crucial in figuring out how much to spend on your marketing efforts toward your prospects.

The lifetime value is the prediction of economic value a customer brings to the entire future relationship with a business. If you have done a good job taking care of your customers in the past, and your products have performed well for them, they are usually willing to give any addition to your product line a try. Because the relationship is in place, far less (expensive) selling is required. Studies show that it costs ten times more to generate a new customer than to maintain an existing one.

If you are not remarketing to existing customers, you are leaving money on the table!

Go for a no-brainer upsell: offer complementary products or services. Put a little thought into what your customers are buying and the other needs that those purchases might trigger, and remind customers of everything you offer. Never assume that even your most reliable customers are completely aware of all of the products and services you offer.

Develop programs to increase customer loyalty and decrease turnover. Stay in touch with your clients via email and direct mail. Have a totally separate marketing approach for selling to them.

Shopping Cart Abandonment Remarketing

Shopping cart abandonment remarketing is one of the most profitable remarketing techniques. These programs are triggered by website visitors' behavior: when they abandon their cart, a personalized email is triggered just for that unique visitor.

These techniques are not widely used in the e-commerce sector as a whole, yet they are incredibly profitable. After all, these programs target website visitors who almost purchased something. It's not surprising that a gentle "nudge" proves very effective. In fact, you can recover up to 50 percent of the people you reengage via email with these programs.

Be sure to add a shopping cart abandonment system when you set up your shopping cart system.

Chapter 7

Buying Triggers, What Really Makes People Buy

All human beings essentially have the same mental triggers that drive actions. In order to influence and understand your customers, you need to know what those triggers are and how to utilize them in your marketing message.

All human behavior, at its root, is driven by the need to avoid pain and the desire to gain pleasure. Even when we do something that appears to be painful, we do it because we associate pleasure with the action.

Anticipation

Have you ever noticed how much buzz there is online or how hundreds of people line up for any new Apple product at the store days before it is available for sale or how some Hollywood movies have huge lines at them on opening day?

Why is that?

It's because both Apple and Hollywood build anticipation for any new release. They create a buzz about the release of their newest products or movies way in advance of actually having these ready for sale. They post hints of them on news sites, blogs, and so on, and it spreads like wildfire all over social media, building incredible buzz and anticipation.

So, you need to do what Apple and Hollywood do: start building anticipation and buzz and start marketing your products well before they are released to get people excited about them.

This will trigger pleasurable emotions that people will associate with your product, and they will eventually buy your product when it is released.

Social Proof

As I mentioned earlier, using testimonials from a happy customer, an expert, or an authority figure who can vouch for the product's effectiveness is one of the best ways to knock down buying objections. It's also one of the best ways to give people the reassurance that they will actually be getting what they expect or want. If you have customers who have used or purchased your product or service, ask them for testimonials.

Offering visual "before and after" evidence of a product's effectiveness is a popular tactic, particularly with weight-loss or skin-care products. Using "before and after" pictures or pictures of the results the customer has gotten are also great tools to reassure your prospects.

TIP: *If you have sold on Amazon or eBay, use those reviews in your marketing; the more reassurance you can give, the better. If you do not have any customers yet, the best way to build social proof is by doing a promotional giveaway of a few of your products on your site or on social media, then asking for feedback and reviews.*

Media

A lot of new business owners are in awe of media in general and think media outlets are unapproachable. The fact is, it's a two-way street. Media outlets, such as magazines, NEED new, timely information, as much as new businesses need the free publicity.

Thousands of niche publications and websites out there are looking for relevant content for their readers. Sending a press release for your product to magazines and blogs or even local TV stations can give your product or service a giant credibility boost. Pitch your story to the media outlets with their benefit in mind. Tell them why their readers or viewers would enjoy reading more about you and your company.

Make sure your photographs do justice to you and/or your product. They don't have to be professionally produced, but they must look professional. Having both low- and high-resolution shots is a must: low-res images for pitching and Web use and high-res images for publishing.

You can find many free services on the Internet, but some that work are www.helpareporter.com and www.muckrack.com. You'll receive e-mails listing queries from editors in need of sources and product ideas for their stories. Find one that suits you, submit your pitch, and wait for the good news—it's that simple and that useful.

Once your product or service has been featured, you can use the media outlet's logo with an "as seen in" on your site and all of your marketing materials.

Scarcity

If less there is of something, people will perceive it to be a highly valued commodity, which in turn means they will want to have it even more. Using scarcity to sell your products is a great way to get your customers to buy from you sooner, rather than later.

It's that ageless law of supply and demand. The less the supply is, the greater the demand will be.

If you sell one-of-a-kind products, workshops, or concerts, the scarcity lies in the number of spaces or number of items available or the fact that it is available for only a limited amount of time. Letting your customer know there is a "limited edition," a limited number, or a limited amount of time available to purchase creates a sense of urgency in the sale.

Limited-time offers are among the most popular in the scarcity category, because they really work. Just think about your average car dealership. Practically every commercial is a limited time deal. "Get 0% financing before it's gone!"; "Sale Ends in 48 Hours." Think of eBay auctions: limited-time offers force the buyers to make up their minds or lose out on the deal. Adding a time limit or a countdown clock to your offer can be one of the most effective ways of selling.

There are various companies offering scarcity countdown timers that you can add to the offer page website, even if you have very little technical knowledge. Countdown Monkey and Deadline Funnel are some of the better options.

If you add a time deadline or a number limit, stick with it. How many times have you come across an offer that had a deadline that seemed to "magically" bump ahead each time you saw it?

Scarcity done very well is when a product or the price is changing after the deadline or is simply no longer available or is temporarily inaccessible.

Think about how you can add scarcity to your product or service.

Tip: *Jeff Walkers book Launch has a fantastic chapter on Buying Triggers. If you want to learn more on what makes people buy then I highly recommend that you read it.*

Chapter 7

Expand Your Offer Options

Entry-Level Products

Lower the entry-level cost of people's starting to doing business with you. Having a low-priced, entry-level product or service can help you introduce your line of products or services to someone who is not quite willing to commit to buying your full services or does not yet have the money to buy your regular products or services.

Entry-level products, such as beauty items and fragrances, help luxury brands establish a lifelong connection with consumers at a young age. . . and they can do the same for your business.

What can you offer as an entry-level product to get people to start doing business with you?

Product Bundling

As I said earlier, you need to make your offer as irresistible and attractive as possible. The more value you can add to your offer, the sooner it will sell.

Add more perceived value for your customer by offering several products for sale as one combined product. The more perceived value you add for your customers, the easier it is for them to make up their minds and purchase.

Have you ever watched an infomercial on TV, where they are selling knives or a cooking set and keep adding items to their offer, adding more and more value until it becomes irresistible?

People appreciate bundles, even at places like McDonald's, where they can purchase burgers, fries, and drinks in a bundle—known as an Extra

Value Meal—cheaper than the products would be if purchased individually. All kinds of products are sold in bundles. Microsoft Office is sold as a bundle of computer software, which includes Word, Excel, and PowerPoint. Cable companies offer their channels in bundle packages. Even a music CD is essentially a bundle of songs.

What product or service can you bundle? What other products or services would complement your product? What else can you add to make your offer more valuable?

Overcoming Objections

As I mentioned before, in any given market, buyers will have objections when buying products. One of your most important skills as a salesperson is to know how to overcome those objections, but online you really are not lucky enough to be in front of your customers to help them overcome those objections.
No matter whether their objection is price, fear, trust, or timing, you need to use your sales message to address their objections so that these are taken care of with your sales copy or in your sales videos.

Planning will be your best ally in overcoming objections. Make a list of all of the concerns and objections someone could have for doing business with you, and answer and break down the objections to all of these issues in your sales messages.

Buyers want to be sure they are making the right decision. The more objections and concerns you can remove, the sooner you will be able to convert prospects into clients.

Chapter 7

FAQ

Have an FAQ page (frequently asked questions) on your website that can answer any specific concern and/or objection people may have about your product or service. The more questions and concerns you can answer for them before they buy, the more they will be reassured that your product or service will fill their need or solve their problem.

Explaining exactly what your offer can or can't do in your FAQ can eliminate many customer service issues, such as returns and negative feedback, and can also assure your customer that the product or the service you are offering is a good fit.

FAQs are a great place to include all of the copy and features that you would normally not want to include in your regular marketing copy.

The better the fit your product or service is for them, the happier your customers will be. Never overstate or overpromise what your product or service can deliver, because the quickest way to erode any trust and get bad reviews online is by not living up to your promise.
Think of a list of objections that someone could have for buying your product or service, such as price, quality, value, or ease of use, and address them by answering these directly in your FAQ section.

Removing Risk

Take the customer's risk out of purchasing from you, it's one of the most powerful purchase motivators out there.

How many times have you bought something that you did not really need, and you thought you could make up your mind later, because the store or the site had a very generous return policy?

Buyers want to be sure they are making the right decision. Unfortunately for them, any purchase decision comes with risk. The key is to make the way you sell to your prospects as easy and risk free as possible for them. Think of the conversations they are having in their heads, think about why they are resisting your offer, and knock down those resistance barriers, by addressing them in your sales copy.

How can you offer to take the risk out of buying your product? Could you offer a full money-back guarantee? Can you give people a week-long trial period? Could you do what Zappos does and let people see if your product is a fit and then offer free shipping and returns?

What could be holding your customers back from accepting your offer? What could their worries be? What could their concerns be? Could it be price? Could it be fit? Could it be that they have tried other products before that have not worked for them?

Guarantee and Trial Periods

To help people gain more trust in your product or service, you should always offer some kind of a guarantee. For example, you may offer a "30 Day Money Back," "No Questions Asked," "100 Percent Satisfaction Guarantee" to a "Low Price Guarantee" or a free trial period in order to take the risk out of purchasing your product or service.

The less risk that prospects see in doing business with you, the sooner they will buy, because you're adding peace of mind to the shopper's experience.

A strong money-back guarantee is an incredibly powerful sales and marketing tool. Offer a strong guarantee, and display it in all of your advertising. If your competition offers a guarantee, do everything you can to make your guarantee stronger.

But most important of all, if you offer a guarantee, follow through on it! As in your sales message, do not promise something you can't or will not follow through on. It will erode your hard-earned trust, and word will spread quickly that you do not honor your promise.

Interestingly, my refund rates are lower among customers who have purchased physical products than virtual products. If you offer a digital product, it's a good idea to include a physical product such as a CD or a book that you ship to your client, in order to cut down on the refund rate.

Security Trust Badges

An additional layer of trust can also be added by getting the security of your website verified and by placing the security badges in very close proximity to the credit card fields on the checkout page. This way, customers are reminded that the form is secure at the exact time they start to worry about security—it's a strategically placed symbol of credibility to soothe the anxious customer. Furthermore, by placing them close to the credit card input fields and not in a generic place, such as the header or the footer, the site is also implying that the verified security logo applies to those fields in particular.

It's a good idea to display your actual physical address and contact information clearly visible on each page of your website, especially on the shopping page, in order to show that you are actually a real business. Make it easy to find phone numbers and any contact information, and be sure to answer any emails or questions quickly.

Executive Summary

TOP TEN TAKEAWAYS

1. All of your marketing messages should have been created to join a conversation your target customer is already having in his or her head.
2. Remarketing is one of the key online and offline techniques to boost sales conversion rates.
3. Have a "unique selling proposition."
4. Take the customer's risk out of purchasing from you; it's one of the most powerful purchase motivators.
5. Having a low-priced, entry-level product or service can help you introduce your line of products or services.
6. Bundle products to add more perceived value. Think infomercial!
7. Build anticipation for your product launches by adding a pre-launch phase, just as Apple and Hollywood do.
8. An additional layer of trust can be added by getting the security of your website verified and by placing the security badges on the pages.
9. Using testimonials from happy customers is one of the best ways to knock down prospects' buying objections.
10. Remove objections with your marketing copy and your FAQ.

Chapter 7

SIMPLE ACTIONS TO TAKE

- Create and implement a unique selling proposition for your business.
- Remarket to all customers using email, retargeting, and sales cart abandonment systems.
- Add entry-level products and bundle products into your product lineup.
- Plan pre-launches for your new products. Think Hollywood!
- Remove buying objections by addressing concerns in your copy and FAQ sections.

NOTES:

Chapter 8: The Raving Fan Customer

The most expensive thing you can do as a business is to acquire new clients. For most businesses, the easiest way to make additional money is to continually better serve the customers you have and make them raving fans of your company, product or service!

In this chapter, we are going to look at what it takes to turn prospects into raving fan clients who will keep coming back to do business with you over their lifetime. We will look at how you can improve all of the interactions your customers have with you by examining the different touch points of the sales sequence.

Creating Raving Fan Customers

In order to create raving fan customers, you need to make your clients become advocates of your business by focusing on delivering to them the best customer experience possible, so that they would never consider taking their business elsewhere. Businesses with raving fans not only offer an exceptional product or service, they also provide an exceptional customer service experience.

It's not just about being different; it's about giving your customers so much value that they can't help but tell others about it with genuine enthusiasm and excitement. You and everyone on your team must be committed to doing whatever it takes to make sure you have raving fan customers.

You may already have heard the legendary stories about how companies such as Zappos and Apple or Amazon take care of their customers, by going beyond the normal call of duty to deliver a superior buying experience, by creating a structure and a system that let them deliver a FANtastic customer experience every single time. You, too, can create a structure and a system that allow everyone in your organization to consistently surpass your customers' expectation.

So, what can you do to convert your clients into raving fans?

Remember what I said earlier about business and selling being a relationship, and just as in any relationship, you need to give it your full attention. You need to give your client your fullest attention at all times, from the moment you meet your dream client all the way through to the sale, in order to do further business together and grow together.

What you need to do from now on is look at all of your interactions with your customers, from the way you attract customers to the sale to what happens during the delivery, and what you do after you have sold to them. You will need to examine every point where you come in contact with your prospects and clients and see how you can design an experience that attracts your dream customer and converts him or her into a raving fan for life.

If you have ever gone to an Apple Store or visited a Four Seasons hotel or a Nieman Marcus retail outlet, you probably know exactly what a great orchestrated customer experience looks like.

Let's take Apple as an example, because this company is a master at providing an orchestrated customer experience. Everything from the way the Apple Store looks to the way it's set up, from the way the sales reps greet you when you walk though the door, asking you the reason for your visit, all the way to the checkout and how they ask whether you would like your receipt printed or emailed to you, has clearly been thought out and designed.

Apple pays attention to every touch point of interaction along the way, from how the reps will help you set up your new device right in the store to the way their items are packaged, all the way to their follow-up with you by email a few days after you have bought a device from them to make sure you are getting the most out of it and to offer you accessories for it. Every single step has been carefully designed and thoroughly thought of in advance and is executed to perfection every single time.

Every touch point that you have with Apple is clearly set up to make you feel taken care of and to make it easy and a pleasure for you to do business with that company.

Designing Your Customer Experience Touch Points

The best way for you to design a FANtastic customer experience is by doing something I learnt from Dean Jackson, which is listing each and every touch point you will have with your clients in the time before, during, and after a sale. Then construct and continually optimize a sequence around these points that will deliver the best experience for your customer.

You want to design it to make your customers feel so taken care of, they will want to continue to do business with you and with no one else.

We have all, at one time or another, experienced fantastic service, either at a store, a restaurant, or a hotel or on a website, where we have been so impressed by how and what the company delivered that it made us recommend it to others. You will need to do the same for your business.

Think of an experience that left you impressed and then think of how that experience was designed and orchestrated.

What were the touch points of that experience? What did they do to attract you to their business in the first place? Was it an offer? Was it an ad? Was it an email? Was it a client of theirs? What set that company's service or product apart from the other offers? Was it what the company delivered or how it was delivered? What did the company do after you did business with it? What made you a fan of that company?

Pre-Sales Touch Points

During the pre-sale touch points, we will look at everything that you're going to do to find the people who want to buy your product or service. Here you will design a way to compel them to visit your website or online store and decide how you are going to convert those leads into paying customers.

You have already done a lot of this. You designed your website to match your dream client's demographics and made offers that compel people to give you their email address, because you gave them a free report, book, trial period, or sample of your product or service that was of great value to them.
How can you make this experience even better? How can you make it more personal? What can you add to give even more value to your prospects?

What can you model from great companies and experiences you have had with them, and how can you offer something similar to your customers? What can you do that will set you apart from everyone else out there? What will set you apart from your competition? What do you want your customers to remember about your company?

During-Sales Touch Points

Once you have persuaded someone to buy from you, you really need to focus your efforts on giving your customers even more value and benefits by over-delivering on your promises.

This where you will provide world-class service that sets you apart from all of the others. One of the main keys to creating raving fan clients is to deliver MORE than you promised and much more than your client ever expected. It is that simple, but very few companies do it.

Delivery Touch Points

First and foremost, deliver exactly what you promised and deliver it by the date you promised it. By doing this alone, you will have a happy customer. When you don't give customers what you promised, you lose them to competitors. But by going a few extra steps and delivering more than you promised and before you promised it, you will end up having a raving fan customer who will stay with you for life and will tell others about the product or the service.

Most important, never deliver less than what you promised! I can't stress this enough, but for some reason, people still do not get this! Many times, I have been promised a product or a service that claimed to solve a problem or do something, and it simply did not deliver what it promised. As a result, I never do business with that company again and will do everything possible to warn others about it, on the Internet and elsewhere.

Always try to be understated, do not offer what you can't deliver, do not promise what you can't deliver. ALWAYS, ALWAYS deliver more than you promise! Deliver 110 percent, 100 percent of the time!

You can do this simply by adding small bonuses to every order you send out. If you are selling information products or books, include some extra information on a bonus CD or DVD or add access to a special resources Web page. If you are selling a clothing product, you could add a small mending kit. If you have a beauty product, add a small sample of another of your products. If you are selling edibles or cookware, include some recipes. It doesn't have to be anything big or expensive, but it should be complementary to the product or service that you delivered. Small gestures go a long way.

One of the simplest, cheapest, and most effective ways to let your customers know you care is by including a simple handwritten note with their order, thanking them for their purchase and letting them know they can contact you if they need any help. This simple act will make you stand out from the crowd and adds a human touch to a digital experience.

TIP: *If you are shipping your product, one of the easiest ways to make your client happy is by simply bumping up the speed of delivery one grade to either second day or next day service, in order to impress your clients and make them happy. Zappos, the online shoe store, usually does this to all of its orders. Zappos' motto is "Powered by Service." I highly recommend that you read Delivering Happiness by Tony Hseih. It's a fantastic book about how he founded Zappos and created the company's philosophy.*

After-Sales Touch Points

Most people think the most important part of the sales process is over once they have delivered their product or service. By setting up extra touch points beyond the actual sale, you create a customer experience that sets your product or service apart from most others out there.

Once you have shipped and delivered, always follow up with your customers to make sure they received everything they expected from your product or service. Just by adding this touch point, you can ensure that your client feels taken care of, you can make sure you have delivered what your client expected, and you can avoid any problems that may have arisen.

Do this by using your CRM (Customer relationship management system) or email autoresponder or, even better, by calling the customer in person over the phone.

One of the most important aspects of delivering a world-class customer experience is how you address problems when they arise. No matter how well you plan, no matter how good your product or how professional your service is, sometimes things just go wrong.

It is of utmost importance to quickly address any problems. Put yourself into the customer's position and see how you can best resolve the issue from his or her point of view. What would the best solution be for the customer? What would be most beneficial to that person? What would solve the customer's problem the fastest?

Most of the time, a detailed FAQ page on your website can solve small questions or problems that could arise. Display the solution to issues that are due to improper use on the FAQ page, along with how-to videos, so that minor problems can be solved easily by the customer, without the customer having to call or contact you and saving everyone involved lots of time and aggravation. Anticipate any problems that could arise beforehand, and you will solve many problems later down the road.

Make sure that it's easy for your customer or client to contact you. Be sure that all of your contact information is clearly visible on your website's pages, in emails, and on invoices. Don't forget to include all of your contact information in the FAQ section!.

If something gets lost or damaged in delivery, send out a replacement right away. If customers don't get what they expected from the product or the service, find a way to make it work for them by any means you can, so that they get the results they desire. Even if you have to upgrade the customer to a different product, it may cost you bit of money on that sale, but you will gain a lifelong customer.

One of the biggest mistakes you can make is to ignore or be slow in your response to addressing a fix for someone who has a problem. We live in the age of instant communications, where one can no longer hide dissatisfied customers, because they can post negative reviews on the sites where you have it listed, tweet about it on Twitter, or post nasty comments on a Facebook fan page. It is of utmost importance that you immediately address any problem a customer has and in the best way, always favoring the customer.

If, for some reason, you are unable to resolve a customer's problem, offer a FULL refund, including shipping, right away, no further questions asked! Your time and effort are better spent helping other customers and delivering amazing service to them. But keep track of all problems, and make sure you address the issues so that you can avoid them in the future.

Don't forget that you can always use online and offline touch points to engage your customer. After you have made the sale, you will have the customer's physical address and telephone number, so now you can call your customer, you can send him or her mail, thank-you cards, birthday cards, season's greeting cards, and so on. Use this information to your advantage to connect with your customers on a deeper level.

Testimonials and Referrals

Building your business, one happy customer at a time, is fun and fulfilling. One of the first things you should do after you have served clients and made sure that they are happy with what they received is to get a testimonial and referrals.

It's always amazing how many people simply do not do this or forget to do this step. Remember, a happy customer will tell two or three people about a positive shopping experience; those two or three people could become your customers simply by asking your client to refer someone else whom they know would benefit from your product or service and then following up on that lead. It is that simple.

You can do this in person, via a phone call, or you can automate the process by having an automated email sent to your clients, asking them for a testimonial and a referral.

Setting Up Your Touch Points

What I want you to do now is think about which touch points you can add to your sales sequence in the before, during, and after periods of a sale sequence, so that you will give your customers a world-class customer experience.

How can you attract the dream customers you want? How can you engage during the pre-sale? What touch points can you add? What are the during-sale touch points in your business, and what points could you add? What are your post-sale touch points going to be?

You need think about this in detail. The more you plan the sequence and the more you anticipate your customers' needs, the better you will be able to serve your customers.

Think of every detail you could add that would making working with you or using your product the best experience for your customer. Think of how you can really take care of your customers in a way they would want to be taken care of, after they have bought from you.

Make your entire sales sequence easy, and make it a pleasure for customers to do business with you. Think of the amazing customer service experiences you have had in the past, think of what made them special to you, and see how you can model those experiences and can adapt them to your business.

Above all, deliver a world-class experience!

Chapter 8

Executive Summary

TOP TEN TAKEAWAYS

1. Offer a unique way of selling that sets you apart from all of the others.
2. It's not just about being different; it's about providing so much value that your customers can't help but tell others about your product or service with genuine enthusiasm and excitement.
3. First, deliver at least what you promised by the time you promised it; that will give you a happy customer. Go the extra step of delivering more than you promised.
4. Add small bonuses and handwritten notes in each order.
5. Once you have delivered, always follow up with your customers to make sure they received everything they expected from your product or service.
6. One of the first things you should do after you have served clients and made sure they were happy with what they received is to get a testimonial and referrals.
7. Make it easy for your customer or client to contact you. Be sure that all of your contact information is clearly visible on your website, emails, and invoices.
8. If, for some reason, you are unable to resolve a problem for a customer, offer a FULL refund, including shipping, right away! No questions asked!
9. Don't forget that you can always use online and offline touch points to engage your customer. Once you have made the sale, you will have the customer's physical address and telephone number. Use them!
10. Design your entire sales sequence so that it becomes easy and a pleasure for customers to do business with you.

SIMPLE ACTION STEPS TO TAKE

- Make sure you always deliver what you promise.
- Write down all of the touch points your customers have when doing business with you.
- Design a sequence to deliver the best service around those touch points.
- Always deliver more than you promised. Find small gifts that would complement your product and add them to your order as gifts.
- Add personal handwritten notes to your orders.
- Always deliver a world-class experience!

NOTES:

Statistics show that 90% of people don't read past the first chapter of a book. Congratulations, you're in the top 10%! Don't let this new knowledge go to waste.

The 30 Day to Making Money Online Workbook will walk you through each step covered in this book, so you take the actions you need in order to succeed online.

The digital workbooks are available online for only $19.99 at: www.internetsalesmastery.com/workbook

Once you have read the book, we highly recommend that you download the free Bonus PDF sheets online at: www.internetsalesmastery.com/bonus

We'd really love to hear from you and get your feedback on our products, as well as learn about your results, so please contact us at: feedback@internetsalesmastery.com

Acknowledgments

This book would not have been written if I had not had the great help, inspiration or support of these great people:

Aaron Hinde, Adam Grant, Aj Mihzad, Alana Love, Ale Sueldo, Alex Charfen, Alex and Mimi Icon, Andrew Tang, Anil Gupta, Anna Manjavacas, Ari Meisel, Arriana Huffington, Arun Sarawat, Barry McKinnley, Ben Greenfield, Bernarda Lobo Perez, Bill Arning, Billie Sandoval, Bo Eason, Brad Starks, Brad Starks, Brendon Burchard, Brian Rose, Cameron Herald, Caty Piqueras, Chip Franks, Chris Plough, Cristian Aranciba, Dadapani, Dale Mincey, Dan Kuschell, Dawn Watson, Dean Graziosi, Dean Jackson, Deborah Battersby, Deepak Chopra, Denise Ward Gosnell, Dieter Lutz, Don Luis Pinedo, Dona Agrizzi, Dr Amon, Dr Sean Stephenson, Dr. Andrew Weil, Ed Swain, Eelco De Boer, Ethan Willis, Fenecz Müller, Fernando Kahn, Frank Kern, Frankie Mirandes, Freddy Frisuelos, Gary King, Gil Serique, Gilles Bensimon, Giovanni Marsico, Heather Esposito, Hitesh Haria, Howard Tiersky, Ivonne Salcedo, J.P. de Joria, JJ Virgin, JP Sears, Jamil Lila, Jason Harris, Jayson Gaignard, Jeff Hays, Jeff Walker, Jim Kwick, Jimmy Harding, Joachim Kantenwein, Joan Rosenberg, Joe Cororan, Joe Foley, Joe Polish, Joel Weldon, Joey Coleman, Jon Goodman, Jon Levy, Jon Veytia, Jordan Harbinger, Kevin Donahue, Kevin Thompson, Kevin Thompson, Kyle Witt, Linda Indira Shekterian, Marcela Rey, Mari Umpierre, Marissa Brassfield, Matt Curry, Mel H Abraham, Mike Cline, Mike Koenigs, Mikhail Baryshnikov, Monica Balmaceda, Mother Teresa, Nicholas Kumich, Nick and Rick Swope, Nik Tarascio, Nir Eyal, Pepper Forman, Peter Daimandis, Peter Müller Peter, Renee Airya, Richard Tripp, Rick Ross ,Rob Scally Pope, Robin Robins, Rodrigo Machado, Roland Gebele, Russell Brunson, S.N.Goenka, Stephen M Key, Steve Engle, Steve Glanstein, Steve Sims, Sylvain Corrodi, T Harve Ecker, Tad Schinke, Thadalius Gala, Tim Darwish, Tom Pressgrove,Tony Robbins, Tucker Max, UJ Ramdas, Usha Patel, Velu Raman, Victor Rivero, Vince Di Marco, Vince and Jo Stanley, Walter Freiberg, Wilfredo Vazquez, Willard Bath, Yogi Saras my editor Patricia Waldygo and Chris Wright who narrated the audio books.

Index

AdsManager **136**
Advertising 111, 128, 129
After-Sales **173**
Alexa 58, 59, 66, 84, 89
Alibaba 72
Amazon 43, 46, 48, 51, 55, 58, 67, 68, 69, 72, 78, 83, 117, 151, 156, 168
Anticipation **155**
Apple .... *See*
Audience Insights 55, 57, 66, 84, 95, 118, 129
Automation 98, 99
autoresponder 99
benefits .4, 67, 76, 91, 98, 107, 108, 112, 114, 115, 122, 171
Blendtec 42, 84, 86, 89, 122
bullet points 90, 112, **113**, **114**, **115**, **156**, **164**
Bundling **159**
call to action 85, 106, 114, 115, 116, 122, 130, 142, 145, 146
campaigns **126**, **134**, **143**, **146**, **147**, **152**
ClickBank 45, 67, 69
CLV 153
Colors 95
comfort zone 29, 30, 31, 37, 38
Competitors 90
control offer **116**
Corbis 97
CPC 129, 131, 134, 135
Craigslist 45, 71
CRM **99**, **173**
Crowdfunding 70
CTA **114**, **115**
customer avatar 54, 60, 61, 63, 64, 66, 81, 82, 141, 147
Customer Experience **169**
Customer Service 74
CustomInk 70
Design 12, 93, 95, 97, 127, 177, 178
DollarPhotoClub 97
Domain Name 91

eBay 1, 2, 3, 67, 69, 72, 78, 117, 156, 158
Elance 67, 71, 97
Email 98, 101, 137, 141
Entry-Level Products **159**
Etsy 69, 117
Existing Customers **153**
Facebook ... 49, 50, 51, 55, 56, 57, 58, 59, 65, 66, 71, 84, 95, 105, 118, 119, 120, 123, 124, 128, 129, 130, 132, 136, 141, 146, 147, 152, 174
FAQ **90**, **161**, **164**, **165**, **174**
feedback 33, 75, 76, 79, 126, 127, 156, 161
Goal 25
GoDaddy.com 92
Google 2, 41, 42, 43, 44, 46, 48, 50, 51, 54, 55, 56, 58, 65, 71, 82, 83, 84, 91, 97, 120, 121, 122, 123, 131, 132, 135, 136, 141, 146, 147, 152
Guarantee 113, 162
headline 76, 109, 110, 116, 121, 130, 131, 138
HootSuite **126**
hosting 82, 92, 93, 101
Images 42, 50, 51, 65, 97, 130
Indiegogo 70
Instagram 105, 124
Irresistible Offer 110
iShopping Cart 98
iStock 97
Item Descriptions 73
Key Question 16, 18, 19, 38
keyword 42, 44, 56, 74, 82, 91, 122, 132, 134, 135
Kickstarter 70
Landing **142**
LinkedIn 119
local 2
marketing 6, 53, 54, 56, 57, 59, 60, 61, 63, 67, 74, 82, 86, 95, 98, 101, 103, 104, 108, 113, 116, 117, 121, 122, 124, 136, 137, 138, 140, 141, 143, 144, 145, 146, 147, 149, 150, 152,

Index

153, 154, 155, 156, 157, 161, 162, 164, 185
Media..**125**, **156**
Message..............................109, 127, 139
niche 41, 45, 46, 48, 49, 50, 51, 65, 68, 69, 79, 82, 83, 118, 123, 146, 147, 156
objections 111, 112, 150, 156, 160, 161, 164, 165
offline marketing...............................**144**
Oneload **126**
Paid Search **131**
payment systems 82
PerfectAudience 136
Performance Tracking.......................**143**
photographs 74, 85, 101, 157
Pinterest 123, 124
Post-Sales..74
Question.....................................17, 18
questions 3, 9, 11, 13, 14, 15, 16, 17, 18, 37, 49, 61, 63, 75, 79, 90, 108, 111, 112, 123, 141, 151, 161, 163, 174, 177
Quirky..69
Raving Fan **167**
Reengaging **140**
Referrals **175**
Remarketing..................**152**, **154**, **164**
Retargeting **136**
reviews ...**43**, **46**, **48**, **66**, **75**, **76**, **79**, **90**, **113**, **114**, **124**, **133**, **134**, **156**, **161**, **174**
Risk **161**
ritual 29, 34
Sales Force 99
Sales Message................................104
Sales Process....................................72
Scarcity.......................................157, 158
Security Badges **163**
Selling................**42**, **46**, **151**, **152**, **153**
Shopify..94, 101

Shopping cart..................................... 154
Shopping Cart Abandonment **154**
Skreened 70
Social Media Best Practices............. 125
Social Proof..................................... **156**
Split-Test 116
squeeze page............................. 137, 142
Subject Line 138
success..6, 7, 9, 10, 11, 13, 15, 16, 17, 18, 19, 24, 28, 31, 34, 35, 41, 46, 50, 61, 64, 65, 68, 74, 76, 78, 81, 84, 86, 117, 121
survey 49, 76
TeeSpring 70
templates 94, 97
Testimonials..............................**113**, **175**
Testing 67, 71, 90, 99, 101
Touch Points ...**169**, **170**, **171**, **173**, **175**
Trader Joe's 62
Trafficgeyser **126**
Triggers... **155**
trust 33, 72, 85, 95, 96, 98, 103, 105, 106, 110, 111, 113, 115, 125, 126, 142, 144, 150, 152, 160, 161, 162, 163, 164
Tweetpages **127**
Twitter........................... 105, 120, 121, 174
Unique Selling Proposition **151**
USP..**150**, **151**
values 20, 22, 37, 106
Video.. 115
Vitamix 42, 83, 84, 85, 86, 89, 114
Warrior Forum..................................... 45
watermarks **127**
Web Design 97
why..19, 20, 21, 22, 26, 32, 35, 115, 125, 157, 162
WooPress 94
Writing.. 73
Yelp 124
YouTube.................. 73, 105, 120, 121, 122

Legal

Internet Sales Mastery (ISM) assumes no responsibility for errors or omissions that may appear in this publication. While all attempts have been made to verify information provided in this publication, neither the Authors nor the Publisher assume any responsibility for errors, inaccuracies, or omissions. Any slights of people or organizations are unintentional. Company names and product names mentioned in this document may be trademarks or registered trademarks of their respective companies and are hereby acknowledged.

ISM reserves the right to change this publication at any time without notice.

This workbook offers business, self-help, and marketing information and is designed for educational purposes only. You should not rely on this information as a substitute for, nor does it replace, professional advice. The use of any information provided on this site is solely at your own risk. In particular, you should regularly consult a doctor in all matters relating to physical or mental health, particularly concerning any symptoms that may require diagnosis or medical attention. We and our licensors or suppliers make no representations or warranties concerning any treatment, action, or application of medication or preparation by any person following the information offered or provided within or through the Sites. Neither we nor our partners, nor any of their affiliates, will be liable for any direct, indirect, consequential, special, exemplary, or other damages that may result, including but not limited to economic loss, injury, illness, or death.

You alone are responsible and accountable for your decisions, actions, and results in life, and by your use of the Sites, you agree not to attempt to hold us liable for any such decisions, actions, or results, at any time, under any circumstance.

Earnings Disclaimer: We don't believe in "get rich" programs – only in hard work, adding value, building a real and professional career, and serving others with excellence and constancy. Our programs are intended to help you share your message with a wider audience and to make a difference in the world while growing your personal brand. Our programs take a lot of work and discipline, just like any worthwhile endeavor or professional continuing education program. Please don't enroll in our programs if you believe in the "money for nothing, get rich quick" myth or ideology; we only want serious people dedicated to real professional development who want to add value and move humanity forward. As stipulated by law, we cannot and do not make any guarantees about your ability to get results or earn any money with our ideas, information, tools, or strategies. We don't know you and, besides, your results in life are up to you. Agreed? We just want to help by giving great content, direction, and strategies.

What we can guarantee is your satisfaction; we give you a 30-day 100% satisfaction guarantee, so if you are not happy for any reason with the quality of our training, just ask for your money back. You should know that all products and services by our company are for educational and informational purposes only. Nothing on this page, on any of our websites, or any of our content or curriculum is a promise or guarantee of results or future earnings, and we do not offer any legal, medical, tax, or other professional advice.

Any financial numbers referenced here, or on any of our sites, are illustrative of concepts only and should not be considered average earnings, exact earnings, or promises for actual or future performance. Making decisions based on any information presented in our products, events, services, or website should be done only with the knowledge that you could experience risk or losses, just as with any entrepreneurial endeavor.

Use caution and always consult your accountant, lawyer, or professional adviser before acting on this or any information related to a lifestyle change or your business or finances. You alone are responsible and accountable for your decisions, actions, and results in life, and by your registration here you agree not to attempt to hold us liable for your decisions, actions, or results, at any time, under any circumstance. - See more at: http://internetsalesmastey.com/terms

About the Author

Rolf Magener is a best-selling author who has written seven books, including the acclaimed Mindset Reset Process.

He's a highly-rated keynote speaker and is the go-to coach and mentor for entrepreneurs and CEOs around the world. His companies offer workshops, private coaching, and online courses on marketing, messaging, and sales.

Learn more at www.Magener.com

www.ingramcontent.com/pod-product-compliance
Lightning Source LLC
Chambersburg PA
CBHW020906180526
45163CB00007B/2644